The
Poetry of Boris Pasternak

1914-1960

SELECTED, EDITED, AND TRANSLATED BY

George Reavey

WITH AN ESSAY ON THE LIFE

AND WRITINGS OF PASTERNAK

Capricorn Books

G. P. Putnam's Sons   New York

Library of Congress Catalog
Card Number: 59-13787

PROLOGUE

(*A Creaking Pine Tree Falls*)

A creaking pine tree falls with deadly crackle,
Interring all the humus in the grove;
Then, History, you stand confronting me
A forest vast and dense of other trees.

For ages sleeps of nerves the tiny mesh;
But in a hundred years men never fail
To start a hunt, or some old poacher flush,
And lead the woodsman with his axe to jail.

Then stunning the countryside with rowdy vines,
Above the thicket there begins to loom,
In ghastly corporality of service,
The forest ranger's wooden leg and medal.

With solid wooden tread he creaks.
An illumined forest rises from its dreams.
The invalid's big smile, in full-fleshed cheeks
Of Chinese lantern, now above it floats.

Contain your joy, and answer to the shout.
For he does not, like us, admire the sunset:
He shines with color like a man with gout,
And though he's bright, he's—like the lantern—dead.

1928

"To give a sense of the freshness or vividness of life is a valid purpose for poetry."

—WALLACE STEVENS

". . . surprise is the greatest gift which life can grant us."

—BORIS PASTERNAK

Contents

The Poetry of Boris Pasternak:

8

Boris Pasternak:
The Man, the Poet
and the Theorist
of Beauty

BY GEORGE REAVEY

I. BORIS PASTERNAK IN HIS LIFE

1. *The Poet, the City, and the World*

Russia, since the days of Peter the Great, was a country with two capitals, Moscow and Saint-Petersburg. Moscow was ancient and traditional; Petersburg, modern and European. This distinction in the past often applied to Russian writers. Pushkin and Dostoyevsky and Blok were certainly Petersburg writers; Aksakov and Ostrovsky were obviously Moscow writers. But the distinction between the two cities in terms of tradition and modernism began to break down early in the twentieth century, and we have the paradox of a Moscow-born writer like Andrey Biely proving himself to be not only the most modern of Russian twentieth century prose writers, but also the author of that remarkable novel, *Petersburg*, in which the last days of a whole epoch are portrayed most vividly and cryptically in the most nervous of modern prose.

Paradoxically, too, the tradition of Russian poetry has been revivified by "the most contemporary of Russian poets" Boris Pasternak, who is himself Moscow born. Indeed, in the sixty-nine years of his deceptively quiet life, Pasternak has spent at least sixty-four in or around Moscow. But it is not only this that entitles him to be called a Moscow writer: his poetry is also steeped in the atmosphere

13

and landscape of the Moscow countryside; but if he is a poet of nature, he is likewise a poet of the city. It is no accident that we discover the following double, apparently contrasting but in Pasternak very intimately related image and simile which he uses when speaking of his experience of soviet life as "this unique world. . . . that hangs suspended on the horizon like mountains seen from a plain or like a faraway big city against the smoky background of a red sunset." Or again there is the statement in Doctor Zhivago's posthumous notes: "When I came back to Moscow in 1922, I found it deserted and half-destroyed. . . . But even in this condition, it is still a big modern city, and cities are the only source of inspiration for a new, truly modern art." The city which figures most prominently in his work, both poetry and prose, is Moscow. But that is only one aspect of Pasternak. Another is his outlook and work in the framework of Russian literature as defined by Alexander Blok in 1908 in his essay, *The People and the Intelligentsia*, where he states . . . "the whole of Russian literature which always—from Pan Slavist to Westerner, from the man concerned with social affairs to the aesthete —nourished a kind of instinctive hatred of dry and rigid thinking and aimed at superceding logic."

Boris Pasternak is a Russian poet, a European poet and, above all, a universal poet and, as such, a free citizen of the spirit. Anna Akhmatova, the eminent lyrical poet, has already expressed this feeling in a poem of hers, *Boris Pasternak*, published in 1940, and it will be appropriate to quote a few stanzas from it:

> "The eye of a horse is what he called himself,
> Who glances sideways, looks, perceives and grasps—
> Till soon, like smelting diamond turning fluid,
> The puddles gleam, ice quickly scintillates.

Since he compared Laocoon to smoke,
And praised in song the graveyard thistle;
Since with new clang of strophes shining in
New spaces he soundly filled the world. . . .

Then be eternal childhood his award,
The generous power and loyalty of stars.
The whole of earth was his inheritance. . .
But he preferred to share it with all men."

2. *Family Background*

Boris Pasternak was born on January 29 (OS) or February 10 (NS), 1890, in Arsenal Street, Moscow. He was the eldest son of Leonid Ossipovich Pasternak, a noted painter, and Rosa Kaufman, a concert pianist. Leonid Pasternak (1862-1945), the father, was born of a Jewish family in Odessa, [1] that city of musical prodigies and other artistic talent. He had first some difficulty in establishing himself as a painter in Moscow but, after further apprenticeship in Munich, he returned to Moscow where he began to make headway as a portrait painter and an illustrator. Though not an epoch-making painter and still largely under the influence of realism tinged by impressionism, he managed in his paintings to combine great honesty, truth to nature and feeling. By 1893, he occupied an official teaching post at the Moscow School of Painting, Sculpture and Architecture, which was under the direct management

[1] Odessa, from the same root as the name of Odysseus, the Greek hero, was originally an ancient Greek city. Later, as the main Russian port on the Black Sea, it had an international population, which included a strong Greek and Jewish colony. Pushkin, when in Odessa in 1823-24, wrote the first three chapters of *Evgeny Onegin, The Fountain of Bakshisaray* and *The Gypsies*. Among soviet writers who came from Odessa were Isaac Babel and Valentin Katayev. Odessa is mentioned by Joyce in *Ulysses:* the sailor, whom Stephen Dedalus meets in the cabmen's shelter, claims to have been there.

of the Ministry of the Imperial Court. The School had as its Director Prince Lvov and as its patron the Grand Duke Sergey Alexandrovich, who is mentioned in the last lines of Boris Pasternak's "Childhood."

Leonid Pasternak took up his residence at the School, where he and his family lived for about fifteen years. Here we meet the young Boris at the age of four. In his Autobiography (I Remember) [1] he describes how he watched the funeral procession of Alexander III from a balcony of the School; and he was living here too during the revolutionary events of 1905, which are reflected in "Childhood." By that year, Leonid Pasternak had been elected as an Academician to the Petersburg Academy of Art. Thus, he appears to have established himself in the official world where honors are bestowed. But he was no mere office-hunter. He was respected and sought after by some of the outstanding intellectuals of the day. He formed enduring friendships with great writers, such as Tolstoy, and great composers, such as Anton Rubinstein and Scriabin. His circle of friends and acquaintances included the Russian painters Serov, Vrubel and Levitan, the Austrian and Belgian poets Rainer Maria Rilke and Verhaeren, and many other leading figures in the world of the arts. Painting, music, poetry, philosophy and, no doubt, some politics, formed the main themes of discussion in this passionately artistic household where the young Boris was exposed to mature conversation at an early age.

Rosa Kaufman-Pasternak (1867-1949), the poet's mother, who was also born in Odessa, contributed greatly to the atmosphere of culture and harmony which prevailed in the household. She had been considered a brilliant pianist

[1] *I Remember: Sketch for an Autobiography*, New York, Pantheon, 1959.

and had already made her debut on various concert plat-
forms both in Russia and Austria; but when, in 1899, she
married Leonid Pasternak, she subordinated her musical
career to the enjoyment of family life. Besides Boris, three
other children were born of the union: two daughters,
Josephine and Lydia, and the youngest son, Alexander.
This was a richly illustrated family. The father, in oil,
pencil and crayon, has recorded the youthful sitters in
many poses and at many ages. We can see them all gathered together in 1914, when Boris was twenty-four, on the
occasion of their parents' Silver Wedding.[1] The mother,
though no longer a concert pianist, had lost none of her
zest for music, and there were frequent musical occasions
both at the Pasternaks' and at friends' houses. Indeed, in his
autobiography, Boris Pasternak describes one such musical
soirée as he saw it or, rather, felt it when still a young child.
He was already accustomed to the sound of the piano but,
on this occasion, he woke up crying at the unusual sound
of a trio playing. The importance of this awakening in
1894 was that it formed, according to Pasternak, the dividing line between the unconsciousness of infancy and the
awareness of the budding individual—from then on he
began to remember. The first stirrings of his memory are
therefore associated with music, which was to prove so
essential a part of his creative outlook. Music also provided
an additional link with the Tolstoys, at whose house Rosa
Pasternak often played.

Leonid Pasternak, the painter, was of course very much
involved with Tolstoy as an artist, friend and admirer. He
had not only drawn and painted the sage of Yasnaya Pol-
yana over a period of many years, but had also illustrated

[1] Gerd Ruge, *Pasternak: A Pictorial Biography* (New York, 1959)
p. 7.

some of his works and, in particular, his novel *Resurrection*, which was first published serially in the *Niva* and then as a volume by A. F. Marx in Petersburg in 1900. These "remarkable illustrations," as Boris Pasternak has called them, were later reprinted in the Soviet Academy edition of that novel in 1935, and the originals still grace the walls of the poet's dining room in Peredelkino. Indeed, his father's work provides a rich visual background to our knowledge of the great Russian novelist and moralist. When Tolstoy died at Astapovo, Leonid Pasternak was one of the first to be summoned to his bier, whereupon he was able to do a final drawing of the uncompromising and tormented giant who was now ultimately at peace.

His father's friendship with Leo Tolstoy exercised a considerable moral and spiritual influence not only on the young Boris, but on the whole Pasternak household. Tolstoy's spirit seemed to fill the house and, as the poet says, "his image stalked me through life." If Boris Pasternak has at one point compared Tolstoy to "a mountain like Elbrus," he has himself acquired, as his life demonstrates, some of the granite-like quality and moral stamina possessed by this princely old writer and "moralist, leveller and preacher of a system of justice." Tolstoy had always insisted on that "grain of truth" which would make a work of art immortal. That "grain of truth" had to be implanted fearlessly, and its presence and realization was the best safeguard a writer had against the jealousy, hostility and criticism of others. This is an injunction which the poet seems to have taken to heart and striven to practice not only in his work, but also in his public speeches which, in midst of the ideological rhetoric of the soviet scene, have always been remarkable for their forthright insistence on historical truth and the larger view. It is interesting to note that, in a speech of 1936,[1] Boris Pasternak actually referred to the Tolstoyan tradition of "Exposure"—"The bluntness with which Tolstoy attacks the venerated and accepted conventions." And it was in "this saving tradition" that Pasternak seemed to find a guide, "in the light of which everything noisily high-pitched and rhetorical appears unfounded, useless, and, at times, even morally suspicious." Another injunction came to Pasternak from his father, which was in a sense a paraphrase of Tolstoy's: "Be honest in your art, and your enemies will be powerless against you." These two injunctions have played a determining part in Pasternak's career and destiny as a writer under the soviet regime, and they are also at the root of his *Doctor Zhivago*, which is, in one of its aspects, an exposure of new conventions of falsehood wherever they may be found. And they have also been his steady support in "a world of hitherto unknown aims and aspirations, problems and exploits, a new self-restraint, a new strictness—new trials with which the world confronts the human personality and man's honor, pride, and endurance."

The Revolution, as it did in so many cases, led to the scattering of the Pasternak family. The father, mother and the two daughters migrated to Germany in 1921. Leonid Pasternak was able to continue his career as a painter, and particularly as a portraitist, in Berlin. But the Europe of the 1930's was complex and irrational: after the advent of Hitler, life in Germany grew less safe and more uncomfortable every day. In 1935, the younger daughter Lydia went to live in England (as she tells me), and in a year or two the whole family had settled in England. By the outbreak of the war they were living in Oxford, and it was

[1] Speech at Plenum of Soviet Writers at Minsk. See p. 86.

there that Rosa and then Leonid Pasternak died without having seen their son Boris for over twenty years. The two sisters Josephine and Lydia are still living in Oxford.

3. *Boris Pasternak—His Character and Life*

> *"The eye of a horse is what he called himself."*

Now I shall treat in greater detail Boris Pasternak's life. First of all, I should like to observe that for a writer in whose work the autobiographical element is so important, Boris Pasternak is a very reticent man. He is reticent not in the sense of hiding his opinions—here he is, and has always been, dangerously frank—but in the details of his private life, friendships and acquaintances. His is certainly a classical reserve rather than the Rousseauesque confessionalism which has become the foundation of modern western ego-sensationalism. In both his autobiographical works, *Safe Conduct* and the *Autobiography*, he has revealed great restraint and a mastery of the art of understatement. From them I get the impression that for him life is mainly an aesthetic (and moral) problem which must be seen and appreciated in its quintessence with all predigested details austerely eliminated. Thus, in these two books we are offered only what is essentially significant to Pasternak, but hardly any crumbs for our baser, all-too-human curiosity. He is no French analyzer of the passions in their minute fluctuations and consequences; no Racine, lashing the stormy soul of Phèdre; no André Gide who lays bare his personal problems and dissects his sins. But then—amazing thought!—perhaps Pasternak is not personally unhappy; perhaps he is not introspective; perhaps he sees life whole. And perhaps, too, he fortunately lacks that element of self-pity which feeds the bowels of the romantic agony. His compassion, which is undoubtedly present, is directed outward to either suffering humanity, as his recent poem "The Soul" bears witness, or to the burden borne by women, to which he is especially sensitive, as so many passages in various texts testify.[1] And did he not raise his voice in the 1920's against the prevalent theory of ruthlesness when he wrote "The Lofty Malady"?

> "It exalted hardness and stagnation,
> But tenderness declared illegal."

A universal tenderness and compassion are indeed the keynote of his poetry, as well as of *Doctor Zhivago* and *The Last Summer* where we find the haunting leitmotif of "that last summer when life still appeared to pay heed to individuals, and when it was easier and more natural to love than to hate." This stress on the individual soul, its joys and agonies, and on the divinely human principles is what the soviet ideologists object to most of all.

But his reticence can also to some extent be explained by the environment in which he has been writing. In soviet literature, biography as a manifestation and reflection of individual life apart from social motivations has been on the whole discouraged. The most fully documented biographical material that has been allowed to be published is that centering round the life and activity of Maxim Gorky; even here, however, there are serious gaps, for the documents have been largely selected to justify ideological assumptions. This suggests that Pasternak's reticence in both the *Safe Conduct* and the *Autobiography* is to some degree enforced and conditioned by the possibilities of

[1] See, as examples of this, Serezha's plans for distributing "millions" in *The Last Summer*, and the poems, "The Wide Wide World" and "My Verses, Hurry."

publication. And when he writes at the conclusion of his *Autobiography* that "To keep up the sequence of events I should have had to speak of years, circumstances, people, and destinies within the framework of the Revolution," we can well understand that this might prove too topical a subject, although one of extraordinary interest.

Pasternak is certainly not as dry as his autobiographical sketches might suggest. On the contrary, he is a highly emotional, ebullient and eloquent man, who always amazes by his cordial frankness as well as by his broad humanity and deep culture. Such was my personal impression of him in the 1940's, and such too the opinions of a number of foreign journalists who have interviewed him in the late 1950's. Together with his almost childlike spontaneity and his consistent fearlessness, he is richly endowed with great powers of concentration on the essential problems of his art. But this does not make him a hermit. After his disciplined hours of concentrated writing and meditative solitude, his solitary walks through the Peredelkino woods and countryside, which he has in the past twenty years adopted as his own, he likes to be the convivial host and to entertain company. He has his Sundays at home and, until the dramatic incident of the Nobel Prize award, his doors were open to a wide variety of visitors, at least during the period of "thaw." Nor should we forget him in the character of the lover and family man. The love motif is present in all of his poetry and prose, and we are told that "many women have been in love with him." He has been married twice and has three sons. So, in this sense, he is a well-rounded and fortunate man. And he has, so far, survived many difficulties and hardships and several illnesses, to say nothing of the nervous strain of the campaign against him after the award of the Nobel Prize, when he was publicly called a "traitor," a "swine" and a "Judas," and when for a time, he was also faced with the following extraordinary situation which he described to a German journalist:

> "Maybe they feared I would commit suicide.... My house was a real hospital at that time. They gave me a woman doctor as nurse. I told her she could go home, she need not worry about me. But she did not go. Apparently, she was not allowed to because she was under orders. Maybe they feared I would commit suicide. I was always surrounded by doctors. They even slept under my roof." [1]

Fortunately, this episode, narrated with such candor and naivete, was no repetition of the Chaadayev incident of 1836, when the author of that name was adjudged insane because his views of Russian cultural development did not coincide with the official interpretation.

Before I delve more strictly into the chronological unfurling of Pasternak's sparsely documented life, it might be well to establish a fairly clear notion of his appearance and temperament. My own personal impression of his physical appearance has perhaps become diluted in the general aura of his spiritual impact upon me when I met him: his voice, gestures, face, and the revelation of inner content, form a compelling enough image of an extremely sensitive man who is never without his gadfly and a true poet who is never without his Muse. He is not to be weighed in avoirdupois, because his large head and powerful body are somehow dissolved by the light in his brown eyes and the deep tones of his freshly spontaneous, and sometimes stumbling, voice which is more often than not involved in a musical soliloquy on the intermingled themes

[1] Report in *Newsday*, December 22, 1958, from Hamburg, Germany (AP).

of art and destiny. He is all of a piece, and is ever ready to break into a long steeplechase of a monologue. This aspect of him is curiously Hamletian but, although haunted by ghosts, he is no divided personality and resolves his conflicts aesthetically, without a trace of bitterness. This presupposes great spiritual reserves, as well as a fund of Christian humility and faith.

There are other descriptions of Pasternak as he now is: "a tall grey-haired man ... waving and smiling ... one of the freest human beings I have ever known. ..." [1] Or: "Tall, broad-shouldered, in an open-necked shirt and rolled-up sleeves, with trousers tucked into his boots and cap askew, from beneath which projects a tuft of straight grey hair, he is busy digging with a spade. ..." [2] We also have earlier impressions of him by Russian writers. Thus, Victor Shklovsky, the critic, who met Pasternak in Berlin when he was thirty-two, described him as follows: "He has a head in the form of an egg-like stone, dense and strong, a broad chest, ... Pasternak is always trying to break away somewhere, though not hysterically but, rather, persistently like a strong and mettlesome horse. He walks about, but he really wishes to gallop thrusting out his legs far forward." Shklovsky catches the impetuous nature of Pasternak's movements which were also so characteristic of his earlier poetry. The comparison with a horse is also apt, and more than one writer has used it, including Pasternak himself when, in a fragment of an unpublished novel [3] the boy character (obviously the young Pasternak) is addressed somewhat bluntly as "So

[1] Gerd Ruge, "A Visit to Pasternak," *Encounter* 54, March, 1958.

[2] Michael Koryakov, "The Thermometer of Russia," *The New Review (Novy Zhurnal)* LV, 1955 (New York).

[3] I have translated this fragment (B) and hope to publish it soon.

you're stuckup, you horseface." His long, bony, angular face does indeed suggest the horse, and cartoonists have been quick to take advantage of this resemblance. But the most striking image of this kind comes from Marina Tsvetayeva, the poet in her first enthusiastic review of Pasternak's poetry [1] where she writes:

"...something in his face at once of the Arab and his horse: an alertness, an attentiveness, and at any minute ...full readiness to race away.... A vast, also horse-like, wild and shy slant of eyes. Not an eye, but an *ocus*.[2] The impression is that he is always listening to something, an uninterrupted attention and then—suddenly—a bursting into word—more often than not somehow a premature one, as though a rock had spoken or an oak tree. His speech (in conversation) is like the interruption of a primordial muteness. And not only in conversation, but I can affirm this about his verse with a far greater authority of experience."

We have now looked from several angles at Pasternak, early and late, and are in a better position to have a clearer image of the man and the poet, the rock and the horse, who, in his unbounded love of life, has expressed himself thus in the last stanza of a recent poem:

"Nor must you even by a hair
Retreat to spite your living face,
But prove as quick and, this your share,
Stay quick, the quickest in your race."

4. *School and University*

Having established the man, let us meet the boy and the youth. First, there is the formal discipline: the school and

[1] Marina Tsvetayeva, "The Luminous Shower," *Epopeia*, Berlin, 1922.
[2] In Russian, *oko*, the archaic form for *glaz* (eye), is now reserved for poetic usage. Compare *steed* and *horse*. Here I have translated *oko* by the Latin form *ocus* from which it is probably derived.

the university. Pasternak did not finish his formal training until the age of twenty-three, on the eve of the first European cataclysm. In a sense, he has been able to enjoy the fruits of his education at peace for only one year, and perhaps that is why he was so nostalgic about that "last summer." Anyhow, after severe preparation at home for passing his entry examinations at the Petropavlovsk (German School) in Moscow, he passed instead into the Fifth Moscow Gymnasium for Boys in 1901. The curriculum of this gymnasium was a traditional one, based on the humanities. Pasternak was there until 1908. Two years before, the doors of the gymnasium had also opened to a somewhat younger contemporary of Pasternak's, the Futurist-to-be and the stormy poet of the war years and the Revolution, Vladimir Mayakovsky. But the two men, whose fates were so curiously intertwined, did not meet till the summer of 1914.

After the gymnasium, where he had learned Greek, Latin, French and German, as well as history and literature, Pasternak spent almost six years at Moscow University, with an interlude from May 9 to August 12, 1912, at the ancient University of Marburg in Germany. He first matriculated into the Law Faculty at Moscow University, but then within a year switched to the History Faculty where he remained from 1909 to 1913. Among his subjects of study and particular interest at the time was philosophy which he further studied at Marburg under the famous Professor Herman Cohen (1842-1918), who was an exponent of the neo-Kantian trend. Pasternak has much to say of Professor Cohen and Marburg in both the *Safe Conduct* and the *Autobiography*. At this stage of the studies, Pasternak felt "a wild-hearted enthusiasm" for philosophy, but he also became critical of "the methods employed to instruct

26

them" at Moscow University. As he says, " the history of philosophy turned into a *belle-lettristic* dogmatism, and psychology appeared as breezy triflings in brochure style." [1]

Marburg, of which he had heard so much from his philosophizing university friend, Dmitry Samarin, became a sort of philosophical mecca for him. That was in February. In April, Rosa Pasternak surprised her son by presenting him with the equivalent of five hundred dollars and suggesting that he go abroad for a spell. "It would be impossible to imagine my joy," writes Pasternak. Naturally, he headed for Marburg, determined to lead a spartan life of "bread, sausage and tea" in order to make the money cover his university fees, lodgings, food and travel. Leading an austere life, he managed to last his four months in Marburg and even to visit Italy afterwards.

In Marburg Pasternak found an independent method which "uprooted everything from its first rudiments and built on a clear space." Here for Pasternak philosophy was "unrecognizably rejuvenated" and transformed into an "immemorial discipline of problems." Besides learning "how science thinks," Pasternak was also greatly impressed by the way the Marburg school approached historical development. In this, it was characterized by both "brilliant universality" and "judicious verisimilitude." Pasternak enjoyed his studies, and made an impression on his teachers. He attended two seminars and, as he says, "My papers came off well. They met with approbation." He was pressed to write a final, more detailed paper. "I jumped at the idea and set to work with redoubled zeal." But Pasternak began to notice that he was not cut out to be a

[1] *The Safe Conduct.*

"learned man," that he was attracted by "literary quotations" rather than by the pursuit of knowledge for its own sake. He was not satisfied with pure logic.

The crisis came in July when a Russian girl of a wealthy family—the eldest of the V . . . sisters—passed through Marburg. He had known her for at least six years; he had been her tutor in Moscow where he had fallen in love with her. She declined his desperate offer of marriage. From that moment, Professor Cohen, Marburg and philosophy seemed to take second place; the first was usurped by poetry. His wholehearted absorption in philosophy had gone: "It was the end, the end! The end of philosophy, that is, the end of whatever thought I had entertained about it." The lyrical poet raised his voice instead. There is in *Doctor Zhivago* (page 407) a passage in a speech of Lara's which seems to sum up Pasternak's ultimate conclusions about the uses of philosophy: "I think a little philosophy should be added to life and art by way of seasoning, but to make it one's specialty seems to me as strange as eating nothing but horse-radish."

5. *Pasternak's Artistic Interests up to 1914: Music and Literature*

Boris Pasternak's family background, as well as his own innate sensibility, made art a second nature to him. When he became enthusiastic about music, for example, he did not have to ask, as he says, what music was. In the same way, he became sensitive very early to the new art of his day. As a schoolboy between the age of twelve and fourteen, he was already absorbing, without straining himself, some of the latest currents in both literature and music. In 1904, he already "raved about Andrey Biely, Hamsun. . . ." And these were the days of Biely's early efforts in verse and prose, the period of *Gold and Azure* and the *First Symphony (Northern)*. But Pasternak's first great passion was music, and Scriabin (1872-1915) became his first "god and idol."

The meeting between the ardent schoolboy and the ecstatic composer took place in 1903 when the composer had just entered into his new (middle) period of stress on magic and incantation, a period which was to culminate in his *Fifth Piano Sonata*, his *Prometheus*, "the poem of fire," and his *Poem of Ecstasy*. This is the period of his composition which Boris Pasternak still likes the best. Leonid Pasternak was unwittingly responsible for the meeting, for he had taken a summer house in the spring at Obolenskoye in the country. Scriabin turned out to be a neighbor, composing the *Third Symphony*, or the *Divine Poem*, the frenzy of which reverberated through the morning air and sent thrills through the youthful listener. But it was not only the music, but also the whole elemental, paradoxical and almost superhuman personality of Scriabin that cast a spell upon the young Pasternak. Here, in the music and the speech, were those new accents and stresses which seemed to dissolve the traditional forms of the past into a freer flow of ecstatic possibilities and seemed to offer a different interpretation of reality, like Andrey Biely's prose—a world very unlike the more solidly and rationally founded conceptions of Leo Tolstoy.

The effect of Scriabin was twofold: it encouraged the impetuous and ecstatic streaks in Pasternak's nature, and in practice it decided him then and there to become a composer himself. For the next six years (until 1910) Pasternak, while still at the gymnasium and then at the University, devoted himself to the art of composition, first under Y. D. Engel and then under R. M. Glière. In the meantime, his "idol," who had "renewed our sensation of music" and whom he "loved to distraction," had gone to spend six years in Switzerland. On his return Pasternak performed before him and won his approval. His musical future seemed definitely determined, for he also had the support of his family and friends in this enterprise. This ambition found support even at the gymnasium, for he tells us that "when, during the Greek and math lessons, I was caught trying to solve some fugue or counterpoint problem... my classmates did their best to shield me and my teachers forgave me everything." [1] However, as in the case of his later philosophical enthusiasm, the culminating moment, that of Scriabin's approval, seemed to bring to a head an inner crisis that had been maturing with concealed agony for some time. Pasternak decided that, for all the originality of his compositions, he did not have either perfect pitch or sufficient performing talent on the piano, and suddenly gave up his dream of becoming another Scriabin. Very soon he took drastic measures to cut himself off from the world of concert music: "I stopped touching the piano, gave up going to concerts, and avoided meetings with musicians."

However, Scriabin's image is firmly lodged in Pasternak's pantheon and the Pasternak of 1957 still speaks of him "not only as a composer, but an occasion for perpetual congratulation, a personified festival and triumph of Russian culture." Scriabin's image is also recalled in several of the lines in *Childhood*:

> "One day,
> When the fracas behind the wall,
> Like the tide, did not die,
> And the whirlpool of rooms was immovably tall

[1] *Autobiography (I Remember)*, p. 39.

And the street with gas was alive—
The doorbell rang
And the sound of voices drew near:
Scriabin—it was he.
Oh where could I run
From the footsteps of my divinity!"

It is also evident that Pasternak's earlier poetry and prose abounds in what I might call Scriabinesque effects which I seem to detect in poems like "The Break" (5, 7 and 9), in various music-imaged passages in *The Last Summer* such as: "After dinner, whole trays of smashed and broken harmonies slid downstairs. They rolled down and splintered in unexpected bursts, more rude and remarkable than any waiter's clumsiness." The allegorical tale of the mysterious "redeemer," Mr. Y., in the same novella also appears to contain many veiled allusions to Scriabin not only as a composer, but also a personality and a "mystique." Mr. Y. is depicted both playing at the piano and reading his poetry in a kind of universal synthesis of all artistic effects and exercising an art which "from the whispering frontiers, ... talked of infinities."

As we have seen, by about 1910, philosophy with him had taken the place of music as a "wholehearted" passion. But as we have also noted, literature was already an important element in the background and, like a racehorse that had been reined back, it suddenly galloped forward and beat all the other competitors to a permanent post. I shall deal with Pasternak's literary development in another part of this essay. Here, I merely wish to stress some of the chief influences of his earlier formative years.

At the age of fourteen, Pasternak was already "intoxicated with the newest literature" and was familiar with Biely, Hamsun and Przybyszewski, the Polish romantic and

31

modernist and, during his visit to St. Petersburg, he had attended performances at the Komisarzhevskaya theater. He was always imbibing culture on all sides. Two years later, his horizon was further widened by a visit to Berlin where his parents had gone, like so many other Russians, to escape the aftermath of the 1905 Revolution. Pasternak's father had been in touch with Maxim Gorky in December of 1905 on a matter of satirical drawings for certain radical papers, and now Gorky had become definitely compromised in revolutionary activities and was to be an exile until 1914. Anyhow, Berlin was full of Russians, political escapees and those who thought it best to play safe. The Pasternaks spent a whole year in Berlin, and this was Boris' first visit abroad. "Everything was unusual, everything different." He walked about the streets, "spoke German, tried to imitate the Berlin dialect, breathed a mixture of locomotive smoke, coal, gas, and beer foam, listened to Wagner." It is at about this period, just before and after, that he discovered the poetry of Blok and Rilke. "The depth and beauty of Biely and Blok could not but unfold before me." *(Safe Conduct.)* On his return to Moscow, he came across two books which Rainer Maria Rilke had dedicated to Leonid Pasternak. As he says in the *Autobiography*, he was amazed at "the urgency of what they had to say, the gravity, the direct purposefulness of their language."

His preoccupation with music, and then philosophy, did not exclude literature; and, besides acquainting himself with the works of some of the greatest contemporary geniuses, he also began to lead an active life in various literary circles such as the Serdarda and Musaget, and showed a deep interest in the theories of Symbolism, the leading movement of the day, as the title of his lost essay on "Symbolism and Immortality" (1910) testifies. At Moscow University, he was the friend of a number of rather exceptional and brilliant young men of notable Russian families like Dmitry Samarin, D. G. Loks and Nicholas Troubezkoy, who further widened his perspectives in literature and philosophy. In the circle of Serdarda, he met not only established authors, but also young literary men like Bobrov who was to influence and help him in the first few years of his literary activity. Thus, as a young man, Boris Pasternak found himself in the privileged position of having all the doors of the arts open to him. He had only to decide to which art he really wanted to dedicate himself. He chose or, rather, an inner voice prompted him to espouse the most difficult calling of all—that of a lyrical poet. The urgency of Blok and Rilke had claimed him.

6. *Poet and Tutor: The Last Summer and the War of 1914*

Having bidden farewell to music and philosophy, and finally to Moscow University in 1913, Boris Pasternak found himself in a quandary. His lyrical mood, dominant since that July in Marburg, could not feed him. His parents were not rich, and they had supported him at the age of twenty-four. To send him to Marburg, his mother had to do some saving from her piano tuition; and the parents, it seems, understood his literary ambitions less well than they did his musical and philosophical ones. But now here was a lyrical poet who only wanted to live, think and write. To write the most unprofitable and mysterious sort of thing, at the first glance—the modern lyric. It was time for the poet to live on, and of, his own, but it was not so easy. Ideally, there should have been a patron or a godsend in the background. Instead, Pasternak had to rely for a time on tutoring as his chief means of livelihood.

In *The Last Summer*, we are given some insights into the young poet in the character of Serezha, an aspiring writer, who has also just graduated from the University, taken a job as a tutor in a wealthy family, and fallen in love. Serezha is both simple and complex, eager to experience every side of life, and involved in an interior monologue where he assesses the value of his experiences. He is faced with the problems of love both sacred and profane. He is both passionate and compassionate, easily moved to tears and preoccupied with the agelong problem of human suffering and degradation. He dreams of a miraculous way to transform human bondage into human freedom. He is badly in need of a few hundred rubles, but puzzles how to raise "millions" which he would immediately distribute. Serezha is on the brink of a Raskolnikov situation, but he is by temperament a Myshkin, "a very Christ of passivity," rather than a fanatic. He works out his Dostoyevskian problem in an allegorical form, and the "millions" in the end are shown to produce no radical transformation in human nature. The salvation, which is always potentially there, must be sought in another, more inward and individual way, in which love alone has power to transform.

In the hot and fateful summer of 1914, we find Pasternak as tutor in succession to the sons of two rather different types of men: Jurgis Baltrushaitis (1873-1945) and Moritz Philippe. Pasternak spent most of June and July with the Baltrushaitis family in a cottage on a larger estate, the owner of which must have been a man of substance and might even have been Moritz Philippe—I am guessing here, but the countryside near Alexin on the river Oka is the same as that described in *The Last Summer*, and Pasternak seems to have become a tutor in the Philippe family toward the end of July. The company at the Baltrushaitisses was mainly literary and very congenial [1]. It included as neighbors the Symbolist poets Vyachezlav Ivanov and Balmont. The lilac was in bloom and there was "fish-broth and bathing," as well as literary work and conversation. And there were ladies too. A more philistine atmosphere seems to have prevailed in the Philippe household, if we note the description of the Frestelns in *The Last Summer*. Moritz Phillippe, we are told, was a rich cloth manufacturer of German origin. In *Doctor Zhivago*, Pasternak has depicted a more sympathetic character of a similar type in Kologrivov who showed himself extremely generous and considerate to the young and wayward Larissa. Whatever Pasternak may have thought of the Philippes, he liked their son Walter, whom he describes as "a nice and affectionate boy." He was apparently satisfied with the conditions of his employment and spent a year in two different stages with this family. He was already with them when the war broke out. In August, the Moscow mansion of the Frestelns was looted and partly burnt during the anti-German pogrom. It was then that Pasternak lost "his books and manuscripts." After the pogrom, he stayed with the Philippes in a rented apartment where he had a pleasant sunny room overlooking the Kremlin.

As tutor, Pasternak had plenty of spare time for writing, mixing in literary circles and for adventuring into the night life of Moscow—"One after another, several women on different nights had swum to the street surface, raised by chance and attraction from non-existence." But I shall deal with the literary aspect of his life when treating of his poetic development which had already reached a first decisive stage in 1914.

[1] See *The Last Summer*, New York, Avon Books.

It was an autumn of women's tears as the front began swallowing up the men. "The war was still new and terrifying in this newness. No one knew how to treat it and it was like entering icy water." *(Safe Conduct)* Pasternak's permanently damaged leg, the result of a fall from a horse in 1903, had gained him an exemption from military service —he had already been up before the medical board in July. To judge from various passages in his prose, this exemption worried him. Thus, in the *Two Excerpts from a Chapter of a Novel*, the narrator is at one point thinking as follows: "It occurred to me again that it might have been better if, despite my repeated rejections by the draft board, I had nevertheless got a whiff of war powder.... But my regret was squarely based upon a love of life. I regretted the gap I would feel in my life if, in that memorable hour for my country, I were unable to share in the exploits of my contemporaries."

7. The Urals 1915-17—The March Revolution

At one point in 1914, Pasternak took some initial steps to volunteer, but he did not go through with the formalities. "The place for honest attitudes was the front," the voice of conscience told him. "...the city hid behind phrases like a thief." This is very like Antipov's argument in *Doctor Zhivago*. But, on the other hand, he was assured by friends who had volunteered that the front was "the precise contrary of what I expected." Thus, in spite of this inner conflict, Pasternak spent the autumn of 1914 in the accustomed cultural milieu of Moscow, which "like all hypocrites...led an outwardly heightened existence" *(Safe Conduct)*. The literary scene too was full of surprises and excitements.

But the next two years brought a drastic and unexpected change in Pasternak's surroundings and even ways of thinking. In 1915, while still tutoring at the Philippes, he was able to get away for some time and travel in the Urals and the region of the River Kama. He spent the winter of 1915-16 in Vsevolodo-Vilva in the northern part of the Perm province. In 1916, when no longer with the Philippes, he lived for another winter in the Quiet Mountains (Tihiye Gory) on the Kama river. There he worked at the chemical factories of the Ushkovs and was also for a time "in charge of the draft board and freed from military service whole districts of people attached to the factories and doing defense work.[1] This is the period of "The District Behind the Front" described in the *Two Excerpts* and in the Fardybassov episode in *The Last Summer*. It is also the country that has provided so much rich descriptive material for *The Childhood of Luvers* and, of course, *Doctor Zhivago*. Pasternak's stay of almost two years in the Urals and on the River Kama had a decisive impact on his creative life and it affected his poetry too, as we shall see later. Naturally, we should like to know more about his life during this period, but there have been no Russian biographies of Pasternak as yet, and his own references to these years in his autobiographies are extremely meagre. Thus, for the present, some of his poems and the four above-mentioned and interrelated works are thematically the best sources we have available.

The March Revolution brought Pasternak's stay in the isolated industrial regions to an abrupt end. Traveling on horse-drawn sleighs through the snowy waste and "the depths of the dense forest," the glittering snow of which

[1] *Autobiography (I Remember).*

sent a "cold shiver" through him, he finally reached a railway station and then soon found himself in Moscow.

He was now back in the turmoil of the city, in the midst of the illusions, conflicts and the nascent anarchy of the early days of the Revolution, back also in the center of a new literary ferment. He was on the threshold of a new age, an age in which "the vast figure of Russia burst into flames." It would not only transform his own personal life, but also reshape the destiny of Russia and influence the life of mankind. And the poet who, unlike Mayakovsky, had kept strictly aloof from political entanglements or enthusiasms, and who had always waged a war against the philistine in any camp, was now to find himself obliged to breathe an atmosphere of political slogans and be progressively exposed to political rather than literary judgment. In a larger sense, the best part of Pasternak's biography from now on becomes an inconspicuous but unremitting and difficult struggle to preserve his human and poetic integrity. For the next forty years, his poetry, prose and occasional public utterances are the most important chapters of his life.

8. *Pasternak's Life in the Soviet Period until 1930.*

Unfortunately for the would-be biographer, Pasternak's autobiographical writings contain very few personal reminiscences or details. They are mainly devoted to literary descriptions and judgements. There is a variety of literary data, but even this is patchy. The period of his life we know least about is that of the Civil War (1918-21), of which there is hardly any mention in the *Autobiography* and the *Safe Conduct*.

This was obviously a period of extreme difficulty and danger for all Russians. In *Doctor Zhivago*, we are of

38

course given a vivid picture of some of the trials and tribulations of those years of terror, famine and typhus. Obliquely, the atmosphere is also suggested in some of the poems of *Themes and Variations*, in some of the rather too abstracted lines of *Spectorsky*, the autobiographical novel in verse, and in parts of *The Lofty Malady*. This early stage of militant communism when "all customs and traditions, all our way of life, everything to do with home and order, had crumbled" was clearly a test of mere survival, particularly in the cold and hungry winters when, as Pasternak writes in *The Lofty Malady:*

> "... through the nights
> We never tired of twitching from the lice ...
> And February, in want, was most untidy.
> He groaned at times, and coughed up blood,
> And spat; then quietly went off
> To whisper in the ears of freight cars. ..."

In the Prologue to *Spectorsky*, there is a quatrain in which the poet says:

> "I lived in want. A son was born to us.
> And for a time I had to give up trifling.
> Now measuring my age with sidelong glance,
> I noticed that it had a greyish streak."

In another line he tells us:

> "I was frozen, and there was no fire."

Apart from such lines, which might have applied to a good many other Russians in this period, and the somewhat more detailed descriptions of Zhivago's experiences, there are very few other facets to help us. All we know is that Pasternak was attached for a year or more to the library of the People's Commissariat for Education, as were a number of other writers, and that his poetic activity continued, but at a diminished pace.

In May, 1921, a new soviet period began, that of NEP, in which there was an improvement in the material conditions of life and an attempt to return to a more normal social pattern. It was an intermediate period of compromise, and it is described in *Doctor Zhivago* as "the most ambiguous and hypocritical of all the soviet periods." In this period, Pasternak began to emerge, despite opposition, as a figure of increasing importance in the soviet literary scene; and he also began to be recognized as an outstanding Russian poet among Russian writers and critics abroad. Also, we learn a little more about his private life. In 1921, the Pasternak family—the two sons excepted—had migrated to Berlin. There Boris Pasternak visited his family in 1923, bringing with him his wife, Evgenia, whom he had just married. Within a year a son was born to them. We can see Evgenia Vladimirovna, as E. V. Pasternak, in a group photograph taken on the occasion of Mayakovsky's return from abroad in December, 1925. [1] Evgenia, née Muratova, to whom Pasternak has dedicated several poems, including "The City," she was a painter. In February, Pasternak also spent two days with her in Marburg, showing her round his old University and visiting his former landlady. Professor Cohen was no more. The Germany of 1923 was greatly changed from that of 1914 and, as Pasternak comments in the *Safe Conduct:* "What had happened in the world became manifest to me in the most terrifying exposition. It was during the period of the Ruhr occupation. Germany was starving and freezing. . . ." He recalled his 1914 dream of desolation, "the saddest dream of any I have

[1] *Novoye o Mayakovskom.* Akademia Nauk, 1958, p. 59.

seen." What he had dreamt was a "desolate field and something told me it was Marburg under siege." Pasternak returned to the Soviet Union later in the year after taking leave of his mother and father whom he was not destined to see again. He has hardly ever emerged from the Soviet Union since then. In the next twelve years he was to become a much published and controversial poet who did not flinch before all the rigors of the Stalinist Revolution. There was to be a revolution too in Pasternak's domestic life in the early 1930's and this coincides with the beginning of my correspondence with him.

II. HOW I FIRST DISCOVERED AND THEN
MET BORIS PASTERNAK (1930-45)

1. *The Discovery*

In every generation the world is renewed through pain and joy, loss and gain, outward expenditure and inward enrichment. The renewal of the world is the principle of youth, and discovery is its privilege. No poet is more at home than the early Pasternak in that world of quivering sensibility, which is agonizingly torn, like birth, between wonder and terror—the world of youth and adolescence, the world of creative impressionability. This is the world of his early poems and *novellas*, that of *My Sister Life*, *Themes and Variations*, *The Childhood of Luvers* and *The Last Summer*. It is the ambience of the poem where the fledglings (or the potential singers) finally take wing:

> "Into the dark of melodies
>   They break away from mother..."[1]

Childhood—not just remembered, but vibrantly felt—is the everflowing fount of feeling and discovery which like sunlit spray, dazzles us with its verbally embodied images. Naturally this freedom, ebullience and perpetual sparkle of self-renewal may have struck some drier spirits, or inveterate realists such as Maxim Gorky, as so many fireworks, brilliant but too elusive. But the world, it seems,

[1] Pasternak, *So They Begin.*

should not always be measured with a ruler; nor should we always and only admire our own gravity, but also the radiance and mobility of fire and water, the instable elements which ultimately make stability possible.

Thus, I first discovered Boris Pasternak for my own enjoyment when I was still an undergraduate at Caius College, Cambridge. But it was not enough just to discover him: I then had to share my discovery and give it to the world as best I could at the time. In the late 1920's there was a group of young poets, novelists and critics at Cambridge, some of whom have since made a name for themselves. The *Experiment* group included, among others: William Empson, J. Bronowski, J. M. Reeves, Richard Eberhart, Malcolm Lowry, and myself. We began to publish a review—*Experiment*. As this title indicates, we were uncompromisingly "modern," far more so than our rival *The Venture*, which had among its contributors Julian Bell and Michael Redgrave. We sometimes included guest contributors like Conrad Aiken, whose "Three Preludes" appeared in the same issue as Pasternak. It was in *Experiment No. 6* (October, 1930) that I published my "First Essay Towards Pasternak" and four of his poems in my translation. " 'First Essay Towards...' " How prophetic this seems in retrospect! I must have had a feeling that this was only the beginning. I intended to enlarge upon the theme.

I must say a word about the atmosphere of Cambridge in those days. We were emerging from the postwar years in a century which had been broken in half before its time. There was unrest in the air and a belief in the possibility of the new, but also a great deal of inveterate complacency. The ancient gateways shuddered under the impact of Joyce's *Ulysses*, Hemingway's laconic muscle-men,

Proust's labyrynthine introspections, the phantasmagoria of *Transition* and the *Work in Progress*, Apollinaire's poetic constructions, Picasso's montages, Pudovkin's films, Hopkins' running rhythms, I. A. Richard's analyses, Spengler's elegiacs, Empson's ambiguities, and Wyndham Lewis' continued blasts; and, at the same time, the Cavendish laboratories were chasing infinitesimal atoms and transforming brute matter into energy. But perhaps this world was not simultaneously given to everyone. Perhaps there was another world. Perhaps there were many worlds. In another sense, literary Cambridge was even more the world of Virginia Woolf or D. H. Lawrence in prose, and of Eliot, Pound and the later Yeats in poetry. Indeed, quite importantly it became the rocky terrain of *The Waste Land* with Prufrock grimacing in the background and the *Cantos* pounding their excisions in the foreground. Anyhow, a certain dryness seized the throat of song.

Now I must tell how I stumbled upon Pasternak. All of us could read French; some, Italian or German; but, as a rule, only a few specialists were proficient in Russian. I was not a specialist in Russian either at the time: I read History and then English. But I had spent 1914-18 as a child in Russia where my Irish father had been for some years director of flaxspinning mills, and I had acquired in that way the best possible foundation for the Russian language. However, after years of schooling in Ireland and England, my Russian was rather rusty. Outside English, I read mainly French and Italian literature. And I might add that my Irish father, disenchanted by his Russian experiences, tended to discourage any Russian reading. But my interest in literature, especially in anything modern, knew no bounds; and I soon found myself, after picking up Pushkin and Lermontov, turning to some of the moderns—

Essenin, Mandelstam, Blok and Biely. My natural inclination was to read the poets first, and the Cambridge bookshops were well-stocked with books in all languages, and the latest novelties at that. At first I got very involved in the poetry of Essenin, whose tragic attitude also struck a chord in me. I was feeling very much in the tragic vein myself then, and had elaborated a whole poetic edifice for myself of which Marlowe was the cornerstone. The twentieth century was Faust's twelfth hour. There was also Dante and Rimbaud and the Shakespeare of *The Sonnets*. The poems of my *Faust's Metamorphoses* and *Nostradam* reflect this attitude and feeling. Naturally, hardly anybody understood the experience I was trying to express except perhaps J. Bronowski and, later, Michael Roberts. I was living poised on the brink of a world wavering between disintegration and disaster.

Pasternak, when I discovered him, seemed to have no public face, unlike Essenin had: he was all contained in the movement of his own verse, in the rhythm of the creative act, and this very act of apparently spontaneous creation, and the resulting chain of his images, were what seemed to absorb him wholly. Pasternak's poetry, with its dynamic acceptance of life somewhere at the very roots of growth, proved a natural antidote to the tragic attitude of Essenin, that of the poet in conflict with his age, as well as to the sheer willfulness of Mayakovsky, just as the spontaneity of Hopkins' lyricism proved a safeguard against the calculated balance of Eliot's lines. My copies of Pasternak's *My Sister Life* and *Themes and Variations* still bear the date of purchase, 1927. It must have been toward the end of the year that I bought them. But they took a few years to digest.

Some of Pasternak's early and middle work is no easy reading even for Russians. But then the Irish can be difficult too, and *Finnegans Wake* is a harder nut to crack than Pasternak. During my holidays in Ireland and, in term time, at Cambridge I must have puzzled over many a passage of Pasternak. Though much detail required elucidation, Pasternak's purity of lyrical tone immediately conquered. There was something refreshingly attractive and infectious about the lyrical quality and heartbeat of this poet, and I felt more and more involved in his cascading images and the verve of his protean verbs. It was a poetry that was difficult to pin down or set in any groove. It was musical and exuberant, full of sunshine and storm clouds, and unpredictable as a woman or the weather. It seemed very atomic in its composition; now like a bursting rocket, now like a shower of rain.

> "To love—to walk, and still the thunder peals!—
> To trample on nostalgia, wear no boots,
> To startle adders, and with good repay
> The evil done by cranberries and cobwebs. . . ."

And what is even more important, particularly in the light of later history, one could feel a beneficent power—a love and enjoyment of life, and the need to be constantly reborn:

> "And this is how I sang and died, and sang
> And died again, and yet came back revived,
> Returning to her arms a boomerang. . . ."

In retrospect, this poem of 1917 seems to contain in it already the idea of resurrection which figures so prominently in the Zhivago theme. And earlier in this poem there was an allusion to the Last Supper.

As I wrote in 1930,

> "His sensibility is always of the finest; his craftsmanship hellenic; his lyric impetuous yet reserved . . . a

46

spontaneity tempered with a nice intellectual balance; an unusual vision; and a sincerity; which all single out Pasternak to be, if not the most obvious, nevertheless one of the most remarkable lyric poets of the time."[1]

2. *My Correspondence with Pasternak.*

Now a few words about my personal relations with Boris Pasternak. Acting, I suppose, with all the fatality of instinct, I sent Pasternak a letter and a copy of *Experiment, No. 6*, as well as some extra translations. By this time I was living mainly in Paris where I had also become one of the editors of *The European Caravan*, the aim of which was to survey the European literary scene in anthology form. I must have mentioned this and other projects to Pasternak besides expressing my enthusiasm for his work and my desire to propagate it. Anyhow, the letter and *Experiment* went off by ordinary post to the mythical land of the Five-Year Plans, past all the censors to its proper destination. Of course, the Pasternak of 1930-31 was at least a century older in experience—the experience that lies at the core of *Doctor Zhivago*—than the Pasternak of 1917. There was a delay of some months, but there was reason for it, as I discovered. Then one day in 1931, a long letter dated March 28th arrived from Boris Leonidovich himself. A phantom figure had suddenly become real, speaking in tones of warmth and encouragement, modesty and resolution: "Your translation and article, your attention and your letter besides, have moved me deeply."

Little had I known! I had apparently written Pasternak at a moment of crisis in his life. It was the crisis he refers to in his autobiography when he and his future wife, as

[1] George Reavey, "First Essay Towards Pasternak," *Experiment*, No. 6. 1930.

he says, were left without "a roof over our heads." In his letter to me he wrote: "This winter [1930-31] there were many personal events in my life ... That is the reason for my long silence which has probably grieved you." What had been happening was a domestic revolution, a breakup of his family life. Pasternak had separated from his first wife, Evgenia. The "future wife" was Zinaida Neyhaus, who left her husband, a pianist and interpreter of Chopin, to become Pasternak's second wife. Of this marriage a third son was born in 1938. A little later he informed me that his former wife, Evgenia, and one of their two sons were soon to leave for Germany where, of course, his parents had been living since 1921.

The events of this winter also coincided with Pasternak's discovery of Georgia. Pasternak had first made the acquaintance of the Georgian poet Yashvili in Moscow. When Pasternak and Zinaida Neyhaus both found themselves without a home, Yashvili invited them to stay with him in Tiflis. This visit following the upheaval to the region of the Caucasus was a sort of revelation for Pasternak. The mountains, the sea and the Georgian people, to say nothing of the sophisticated French-cultured Georgian poets as well as the traditional Georgian bards, all captivated him and stimulated a new lyrical phase in his poetry which is evident in the poems of *The Second Birth*. There too he made friends with Titian Tabidze (1895-1937) whose work as well as that of other Georgian poets he has been translating ever since. But by March 1931 he was back in Moscow where he had many domestic affairs to settle.

Pasternak seemed genuinely delighted both with my enthusiasm and my modest efforts on his behalf. Naturally, I was even more delighted to have his unequivocal approval and support, and to find myself in direct touch with an admirable poet and a rare human being. He also seemed pleased to have established literary contact in the West. The problem of his intellectual relations with the West was much on his mind. In another letter, he referred to "his conversation with the West." In the next few years he was to grow increasingly aware that his name was becoming more familiar among western writers and critics, and that it was held in high regard, but he was always careful to insist in his letters to me that he was opposed to any "artificial projection of me in the West." He also thought that the intellectuals, who knew of him only by reputation, might be disillusioned when they actually read him. And he very modestly added that "he did not think that he had as yet written anything that merited attention in the West." He spoke of his earlier prose pieces, like *The Childhood of Luvers*, as trial pieces "on the way to something bigger." In retrospect, it is clear that, in the domain of prose, Pasternak has been working all his life towards a greater novel like *Doctor Zhivago*. But this makes his earlier prose attempts all the more interesting from the standpoint of their intrinsic quality and as historical foreshadowing of themes, character and methods in creative development. In the light of this "something bigger," it is easier to explain the baffling and sometimes galling reticence of the earlier pieces as well as of *Two Excerpts From a Novel*.

"I have just finished a prose piece entitled *The Safe Conduct*," Pasternak wrote in 1931. After enlarging upon the importance of this work for him, he promised to send me a copy as soon as it appeared in print. This book of reminiscences, with its underlying theme of exploration into the nature of art and culture in general, and their significance in the life of an individual, meant a great deal to Pasternak. A number of passages in his letters bear this out. About *The Safe Conduct* Pasternak said:

> "I wished to express in it a few of my thoughts . . . on a number of questions. Some of these questions it was impossible to touch upon. The rest, which I could broach, I probably did not formulate them well enough. The book, when it appeared, was only a third of what I had originally planned."

This may explain *a posteriori* Mr. Philip Toynbee's complaint when reviewing the 1957 autobiography in *The Observer* that "ideas are suggested, but never explored."

The *Safe Conduct* was published at a crucial moment of the Stalinist era and on the eve of the promulgation of the Socialist Realism platform. The history of the book in the Soviet Union was brief and troubled. *Safe Conduct* was very soon attacked, labelled "idealist" and banned. Pasternak was also exposed to a good deal of criticism. In March, 1933, Pasternak wrote: "A second edition of this book was being prepared, but it was banned a few days ago." The first edition of 6,200 copies had sold out so quickly that Pasternak himself was finally left without a copy and had great difficulty in finding one for me. It finally reached me with a dedication of November, 1932, which reads: "To dear George Reavey from all my soul."

Pasternak's great wish was that I should translate the *Safe Conduct* and get it published. Perhaps he did not realize that it was not so easy to launch a "difficult" *avant-garde* author, especially a Russian one, in the early 1930's. I have had some experience in this field, and I knew it required time; but when quality is involved, the time will always come. It might take five, ten or twenty years. In the case of Andrey Biely, the author of *The Silver Dove* and *St. Petersburg*, of whom Pasternak always speaks with enthusiasm and respect, it took me twenty-five years of effort before he was finally published in New York.

In the case of Pasternak's *Safe Conduct*, I was able to make the initial move. The text arrived just as I was embarking on my *Soviet Literature*, a critical and anthological survey of what had happened to Russian literature since the Revolution. I had already planned to give Pasternak's poetry a very prominent place; in fact, I put him in a section all by himself and stated in my preface, "Soviet Poetry," that "Pasternak, the most considerable living poet, remains influential but isolated because of his peculiarly independent attitude."

I had no copies of any of Pasternak's prose then. Fortunately, *Safe Conduct* arrived just in time and I included two excerpts from it. The anthology appeared in 1933 in London, then in New York (1934), Paris and Milan (1935); and I think it helped to draw attention to Pasternak among a wider circle of readers. I must add that, after graduating from Cambridge, I spent some years in Paris where I was involved in various literary activities. I contributed to a number of Anglo-American and French reviews, and I was able to place my translations of Pasternak's poems in *This Quarter, The New Review, Contempo, The Adelphi* and elsewhere. I also wrote about him prominently in an article published in *Cahiers d'Art* (1935). In 1936, when I was publishing under the imprint of The Europa Press in London, I announced among other titles, "Also a book of poems by David Gascoyne, Dylan Thomas, Guillaume Apollinaire, Boris Pasternak and Vladimir Mayakovsky." This is to be found in the back of my edition of Paul Eluard's *Thorns of Thunder*. It was also my firm intention to bring out *Safe Conduct* as a book, but the war put an end to this as well as many other projects.

The war whisked me away from the literary arena for about six years, and in the meantime a new generation of Pasternak enthusiasts had appeared. In 1938, I was already approached by J. Laughlin of New Directions who wanted to publish some Pasternak poems. In 1940, Robert Payne translated and published *The Childhood of Luvers* in Singapore. In 1945, Stefan Schimanski edited and Lindsay Drummond published in London the so-called *Collected Prose Works* of Boris Pasternak. I was still in the harness of war work abroad when that happened. I was very pleased that Pasternak should have found a new and larger circle of readers, but I naturally regretted that I had not been consulted as regards *Safe Conduct* for I had every authorization to translate and publish it and some rare documentation about it.

3. *How I First Met Pasternak*

I first saw Boris Pasternak in person at the Writers' Congress July, 1935 in Paris. I saw him on the platform, and talked to him in the hall, and at his hotel. It was one of his rare visitations to the West. He was in Paris with a delegation of soviet writers who were attending the International Congress of Writers. André Gide, André Malraux and Aldous Huxley were also present. The atmosphere at the Congress was rather heated and tense. Peace and Culture were the main theme, but there was the threat of war on the horizon and war in the writers' dovecots. Stalinists, Trotskyists, Surrealists, Traditionalists, Independents, were all there fighting each other tooth and nail. It was hardly the place to expect to find Boris Pasternak. I had the impression that he was under great pressure, personal and public, and that he had been exported to the West as a sop to moderate opinion. This in itself was clear proof that the name Pasternak now meant something in western intellectual circles and that this fact had been noted in the Soviet Union. André Malraux introduced him as follows! "Before us stands one of the most considerable poets of our time."

In his brief utterance on the platform, Pasternak was poetically aloof and very much himself in what he said: "I should like to speak here of poetry and not sickness. Poetry will always be among the grass, and it will always be necessary to bend down in order to perceive it. It will always be too simple to serve as a matter for discussion at assemblies; it will remain forever the organic function of a happy human being, overflowing with all the felicity of language that thrills in a native and always pregnant heart; and the greater the number of happy men, the easier it will be to become an artist."

This is the Pasternak we have learnt to expect. But physically and mentally he seemed to be laboring under great tension. On the platform he gasped for breath and uttered an extraordinary moaning sound which made the blood tingle and led one to conclude that he must be suffering deeply. From the atmosphere of the soviet delegation and from the look of mental anguish on Pasternak's face, I thought it would not be politic to thrust my attention on him. However, I did see him briefly and left with him a copy of my book of poems, *Nostradam* (1935), which included a poem, "Exegi Monumentum," I had dedicated

53

to him. This poem, written in 1932, might have been specially designed to express the anguish of the unknown:

Exegi Monumentum

To Boris Pasternak

And what if storm should burst in spite this day,
And all the gathered thunders blunder on our head,
And all the floods we read in fables foam
From secret clouds like Time's avenging ghosts;

And if the ocean should toss free its mane,
With raging hooves throw up lost mountains,
And with its fury-foaming mouth engulf
The ancient monuments we know too well;

And if the winds unleashed break ancient order,
Whirl fatal anarchies for empires old,
Clash whips of chaos, slash, pound, sword and drum;

For trees to shrill upon torn roads uprooted,
Or swayed in dirges of dark sisters' woe,
To wail the day of worlds forever stricken.

Pasternak tells us in his *Autobiography* that he had been suffering from a prolonged insomnia for almost a year or from about the time of the famous first Writers' Congress in Moscow in 1934. "To live—what insomnia!" as Pasternak himself had once written. Whatever the cause of the insomnia, he looked most uncomfortable on this occasion in spite of the sophisticated bonhommie of Ilya Ehrenburg and the fierce geniality of Nikolai Tikhonov. In the background of the Congress feast were the Banquo ghosts: past, present and future. And if Pasternak did say, as Gerd Ruge quotes Ehrenburg quoting, "I don't like to watch people eat," when refused an invitation to dinner with André Malraux and some other French intellectuals, he probably said this in full knowledge of what he really meant. The enigma may become clearer if we think of the Last Supper. It is certainly to be regretted that this unique visit to Paris should have been so constrained and hedged about by political issues; but then it is obvious that Pasternak was not born to travel with guided tours, but rather to eat his bread in silence. Almost ten years later, he reminded me of those Paris days when he wrote a dedication to me in a copy of his *Two Books:* "To dear George Reavey, in memory of his verses, books, our correspondence, our meetings in Paris and Moscow and the sunny October morning in Peredelkino at Zhenia Afinogenova's. . . ."

Pasternak had arrived in Paris without even stopping on his way in Germany to see his parents whom he had not seen since 1923. [1] Evidently the Soviet delegation of writers had to travel en masse. However, during his brief stay in Paris, he renewed a precious personal and literary friendship with the poet Marina Tsvetayeva, who, after years of exile, had developed a longing to return to Russia. It has been said that Tsvetayeva was in love with Pasternak. It has also been suggested that many of her traits are present in the Larissa of *Doctor Zhivago.* In any case, as Pasternak tells us in his Autobiography, he set a great store by her letters of which he had about a hundred. He describes too how they were lost during the war. According to him, he did not urge Tsvetayeva to return to the land of her birth, but insisted she make up her own mind. Within the next two years she did return with her husband and children, but almost immediately tragedy dogged all their steps: the husband was swept away in the purges and Tsvetayeva

[1] According to Lydia Pasternak with whom I talked in New York in June, 1959.

committed suicide in the Volga region during war evacuation in 1941. She is one of the "Three Shadows" in the Autobiography. A few years ago there was an attempt, which met with some opposition, to have her poetry printed in the Soviet Union. Pasternak, for one, has the highest opinion of her poetic talent.

4. *The Years of Trial 1936-38*

From Paris Boris Pasternak returned to an uneasy and tortured land, where soon a succession of trials was to amaze the world. In 1936-38, as the atmosphere grew thick with hate and suspicion, as whole professions were decimated, as writer after writer disappeared in the Soviet Union and terror raged in Germany, and Spain became a charnel house, Europe looked worse than any surrealist nightmare. I am reminded of an early poem of my own which began:

> "Tell me that dream I saw when hooded men
> Surrounded me and bound my arms and led
> Me blindfold under blurred and blotted stars
> To mournful music of a dying world. . . ." [1]

A new monstrous hell on earth had come into being. Hellhounds, fanged and clawing, were tearing at the flesh of truth. Wild rumours circulated. Naturally, I was anxious about Pasternak's fate, especially after the disappearance of Isaac Babel, some of whose short stories I had also translated. In the late thirties I judged it better not to write any letters to Pasternak. I knew that people with western associations were being rounded up by the thousand. I also knew that Pasternak was under a cloud while rumour said

[1] Quoted from poem reprinted in *The Colours of Memory*, New York, The Grove Press.

he was in prison. This was the period which is described in *Doctor Zhivago* (1957) in the following terms: "To conceal the failure, people had to be cured, by every means of terrorism, of the habit of thinking and judging for themselves and forced to see what didn't exist, to assert the very opposite of what their eyes told them. This accounts for the unexampled cruelty of the Yezhov [Head of the G.P.U.] period, the promulgation of a constitution that was never meant to be applied, and the introduction of elections that violated the very principle of free choice." It was a period when some of Pasternak's closest friends, such as Titian Tabidze, were swept away.

Some of Pasternak's neighbors in Peredelkino, like the dramatist, Alexander Afinogenov (1903-41), whose widow Zhenya Afinogenova I was to meet later, were under a cloud too. In 1937, Afinogenov, the author of *Fear*, and some twenty other plays, had been expelled, first, from the Party and then, on September 1, from the Union of Soviet Writers, without any good cause, and as a victim merely of the prevalent witch hunt. He was expecting arrest at any moment. It is at this stage of his life that he first mentions Pasternak in his diary. And yet throughout this nightmare, which had shattered the nerves of apparently stronger men, and despite all the terrors of his wife, relatives and friends, Pasternak stood rooted in his convictions, in his belief in life, in his refusal to accept the impossible. And this despite the fact that he himself had been under attack since December, 1936. "Everyone has forgotten me," Afinogenov wrote in his diary, "*except Boris Pasternak* . . ." (On September 14th), the Pasternaks came in the evening. While we all played cards, he sat on the sofa and read an English book. Then he looked through Webster's English Dictionary. His thirst to know more, not to let a day

57

slip by amazes me. He is an excellent example of an inspired man, for whom his poetry is the content of life...Art is his main preoccupation..." Afinogenov notes that Pasternak preferred life in the country at this point and was reluctant to visit Moscow. He also tells us that Pasternak had begun work on a novel. This passage, and the circumstances surrounding it, not only shed a great deal of light on Pasternak the man and the artist, but they also reveal that Pasternak was already at this time engaged upon a novel which was, perhaps, a first draft of *Doctor Zhivago*. In fact, I have now come across four fragments of this novel, which seems to have its roots in the beginning of the century, like *Zhivago*.

Another passage in the Diary illuminates Pasternak's way of life and gives us a further glimpse of his character and moral influence on his friends, for he undoubtedly helped Afinogenov to survive with honor the ordeal he was facing. Thus he writes: "When one visits him, he immediately...bombards one with themes, judgements, conclusions. He does not read newspapers, which I find strange....But he has never gone until two o'clock in the afternoon, as I did today, without doing some work. He is always occupied with books, with himself...And whether he be in a palace or on a bunk in a small room, he will always be occupied, even more than here perhaps, because he will not then be distracted by having to think of money or other worries and will have all his time to devote to reflections and creative work..." And then, summing up, Afinogenov concludes: "A rare example of a rounded and interesting man. One's heart is drawn to him because he has a knack of finding wonderful human words of consolation, not out of pity, but from a faith in better life: 'This better life will come about very soon—it will come when you enter fully into your work, when you will begin to write again, and when you will forget about everything else.' "

During the purge years (1936-38), Boris Pasternak did not fall victim of the purge, despite the rumors. Perhaps he was helped by the fact that he was not a Party member, held no official position, participated rarely in assemblies, was known for his forthrightness and bardic eccentricity, and now lived in the country. Or perhaps it was Maxim Gorky's influence with Stalin that helped to preserve him for Gorky always had the greatest respect for creative talent and invariably championed it, though he was rather puzzled by Pasternak's poetry. Gorky had defended Babel against Marshal Budyonny and others, and it was not till after Gorky's death in 1936 that Babel was chopped down. Perhaps, finally, it was because Pasternak had no personal enemies or simply because he was a very exceptional man who minded his art and impressed everyone by his Tolstoyan fearlessness and regard for truth, which made it possible for him, when his will moved him, to address himself directly to Stalin. In 1932, for example, when Stalin's wife N. S. Alliluyeva died, Soviet writers were expected to sign a formal letter of condolence. Pasternak did not do so, but instead added a rather strange postcript which read: "I join in the condolences of the comrades. On the eve [of the death] I was thinking, as an artist, continuously and profoundly about Stalin for the first time. In the morning I read the news. I was shaken as if I had been on the spot and lived through and seen everything. Boris Pasternak" This statement appeared in the *Literary Gazette* of November 17. The amazing admission that he was "thinking, as an artist, ... about Stalin ... for the first time" and the suggestion of clairvoyance in the rest of the statement must have startled Stalin, to say the least. This incident has led to a theory in some quarters that Pasternak might have cast a bardic spell upon Stalin and thus gained his protection. Or perhaps it was Pasternak's obvious poetic naïveté that proved so disarming. Whatever the explanation, we must be profoundly grateful that he has been able to continue at his work, which is an essential part of his life, to finish his great novel, and also to write several new cycles of deeply moving poems.

However, this may appear too idyllic. But the circumstances of Pasternak's life in the past twenty-five years or more were far from that. "Life with us is terribly hard, and is getting still harder." That was in a letter of 1933 to me. In 1937, Afinogenov notes in his diary:

> "It's hard for his wife; money must be got and some kind of a life lived, but he seems unaware of it all; sometimes only when things become too difficult financially, then he will undertake a translation. 'But just as successfully I might become a travelling salesman,' he says jokingly. But send him on an errand and he will all the same fix his open glance on nature and people, like the great and rare artist of the word that he is."

Soviet writers can earn royalties or get advances, and they can make a lot of money. At the back of Pasternak's situation is the fact that his own work has so far been published only in small editions, which have only once exceeded 10,000 copies—a small edition by soviet standards. These small editions of Pasternak do not reflect the public demand for his work. Second-hand editions of Pasternak are the hardest of all to obtain in the Soviet Union. Between 1925 and 1936 a good number of his original works, both poetry and prose, were published, some of them in several editions. But from 1936 to 1943 not a single edition of his original work was printed in book form. Here cold statistics inform us about his moral as well as financial position. The 1943 volume of poems, *On Early Trains*, was very slight. Three thousand copies only were printed at 1 ruble 50 kopeks a copy. *The Spacious Earth* (1945) was priced at 4 rubles 50 kopeks, and 10,000 copies were printed. This analysis indicates some change for the better, however small, in Pasternak's moral status at the end of the war. His position had then improved. But the Zhdanov Decree of 1946 put a halt to this upward swing. In fact, no book of Pasternak's original work has appeared in the Soviet Union since 1948. And this brings me back to the "hard life" and Afinogenov's comment "It's hard for the wife." Translation became an obvious way of remuneration for him. Pasternak's translations from the Georgian, German and English poets began appearing in the middle 1930's. This aspect of his work culminated in his renderings of Shakespeare's tragedies and Goethe's *Faust* in the '40's and '50's.

But Pasternak's difficulties of the thirties were not confined to finances. Mrs. Zinaida Pasternak was extremely upset not only by the general atmosphere of all-pervading fear in 1936-38 and even more so by her husband's fearless attitude. Pasternak was apparently prepared to make a martyr of himself rather than follow in the general rush of paltry obeisance. In March of 1957, he refused to sign a statement condemning in the usual abusive manner Marshal Tuhachevsky and other Soviet generals who were to be brought to trial in June. We can imagine the tension at home when his wife thought that he had taken leave of his senses and when all the relatives brought pressure to bear on him. Pasternak still refused to sign, but his name nevertheless appeared on the printed document. Another hand had signed for him. He must indeed have thought that he was moving in a kind of vicious circle from which there was no escape even at the risk of his life. The human will seemed to be thwarted at every turn; the human heart could only bear alone: and the human tongue was struck speechless. Pasternak's poem, *The Artist* (1) conveys with dramatic intensity some such experience:

> "With artist's stubborness inborn
> My soul's at home—when he is strong:
> Men's eyes he shuns—of speech now shorn;
> He feels ashamed his books are wrong."

5. *The War Years:* I meet Pasternak again.

And now let me explain my own sudden intrusion into Russia. The war had swept me first into the uneasy streets of Madrid under the auspices of the British Council to help establish a British Institute in Madrid (1940-41). James Joyce and Samuel Beckett, with whom I dined in Paris en route, were to be my last vision of western literature in the flesh for some time. Then I was in London for a few months where I saw something again of Dylan Thomas, Roy Campbell and David Jones. By April of 1942 I was on a boat and in a convoy heading for Murmansk. I was to join the British Embassy in Moscow or rather, at first, in Kuibyshev on the Volga. I could not help thinking of Chancellor and Willoughby, the pioneer Elizabethan travellers to Russia, as we sailed to Iceland and past, keeping a not-so-safe distance from the German-occupied coast of Norway. I arrived in Murmansk on a trawler, having lost my passport, a lot of manuscripts, and my original boat. An air torpedo had taken them and much else down to the haunts of Willoughby. I shall not here describe my first impressions of Murmansk, Arkhangel, Moscow and Kuibyshev. Suffice it to say that I began to find my feet in Kuibyshev, made the acquaintance of the Bolshoy Theater and met a few literary men, including Valentin Katayev, the author of *The Embezzlers*. In April of 1943, I moved to Moscow where a more complex life began. Moscow was reviving rapidly from the effects of the siege, people were gradually returning, and there was increasing evidence of literary and cultural life. I was not in exactly a literary mood for some time to come. I was still under the impression that the poet in me had died and had become reincarnated in another person who wrote drafts, telegrams and memoranda. After the torpedoing, I had nothing personal to remind me of the past. Even my wife in bomb-wrecked London seemed remote. Moscow had a certain charm of its own and an air of hospitality but, even despite the political thaw of the war years, there was a feeling of some aloofness and restraint when it came to human contacts. There were exceptions of course, and a great deal of warmth beneath the surface; but there were also the lingering scars of fear. The shadow of Yezhov still loomed in the background. The purges were a recent memory and who knew about the future? Indeed, the cautious souls were right. Within three to five years the Zhdanov Decree and the "anti-Cosmopolitan" drive were to punish the enthusiasm of the optimists.

6. *In Moscow*

The round of official and diplomatic parties continued; a box in the Bolshoy was always available; the theaters were accessible; the food was rationed, but plentiful (all this, however, was diplomatic privilege, not the grindstone of ordinary life). I began expanding my acquaintances, and life became more varied. I met more literary men and other intellectuals. Speaking Russian fluently, I kept forgetting that I was supposed to have contacts with soviet intellectuals only through the kind auspices of the Society of Cultural Relations or The People's Commissariat for Foreign Affairs where an official or translator did the introductions and sat in on the conversation. But it is hard to maintain any personal interest or human continuity under such circumstances, but I suppose it was personal contact or the possibility of developing acquaintance that was being discouraged. I would have had to bridle Pegasus to keep to such a system. Time is an important factor, and so is the natural curiosity and the friendliness of the average man. Nor was I quite unknown. My anthology of the middle thirties had apparently made some impression even here, for I was often addressed as "the translator of Mayakovsky," and I was soon showered with books from every direction. These proved very useful later when I settled down in London to write my analytical study *Soviet Literature Today*. But at the time, in this atmosphere I could not concentrate very deeply on books.

I met some interesting writers of note: Alexey Tolstoy, Fedin, Simonov, Marshak, Anna Akhmatova, and many others. Where, you will ask, was Pasternak? First of all, he was not in town, but still in Peredelkino. Secondly, he attended none of the functions or places where I had a chance to meet writers. He was not at all in the official swim; and there was still some kind of mystery or strange aura about his name; it was as though he were in a special kind of isolation, half of his own will and half of somebody else's. Having corresponded with him for ten years and having met him in Paris, it went against my grain to ask for an official interview with him which might very well have been refused. However, the inevitable happened. By the autumn of 1943, we were in touch with each other. I even arranged to have him invited through official channels to a party at the British Embassy for Sir Anthony Eden, which he attended with other distinguished representatives of the soviet political, military, literary, theatrical, scientific and art world. I think he was very pleased to come; and this occasion may have eased for a while what he once described to me as "the steady touchiness of my local moral position." The Pasternak of 1943 had already become the translator of some of Shakespeare's tragedies, and his happy labors in the field of English had encouraged him to try his hand at English too, as the above quotation testifies. Elsewhere he writes, "Excuse my barbarian and illiterate English. I do not speak it because I never had the luck of a real practice in it, and I forget and remember it in conformity to my Shakespeare studies and the interruption of them. . . ." Pasternak told me that he remembered me very well though we had not seen each other for some eight rather hair-raising years. I soon got him a collection of English poets and some critical studies of Shakespeare; and later, a volume of Gerard Manley Hopkins.

The German invasion of June 1941 had apparently found Pasternak in his apartment in Moscow where he had just settled down to begin the translation of *Romeo and Juliet*. His version of Hamlet had already been published that year. The war naturally interrupted this labour. His son was going away on defence work and, in these early months of the war, everybody was being mobilized for defence activities of one kind or another. Pasternak found himself acting as a roof-watcher on top of a twelve-story building. There he had the experience of two nearby aerial torpedo explosions. Soon after, his friend Alexander Afinogenov was killed after surviving his "disgrace," in one such explosion in Moscow just as he was about to be appointed as a sort of cultural liaison officer with the allied western democracies. Two years later Pasternak wrote a piece in his memory. In 1941, Pasternak also discovered in the course of military instruction that he was a good marksman. This is reflected in his poem, *Outcast*, where he writes in one of the stanzas:

> "This man's not yet old, nor a figure
> Of fun for men younger in strength;
> And his shotgun is even younger
> By some twenty summers in length."

By the end of October, when the Germans were besieging Moscow and the soviet resistance was better organized, he traveled to stay in an isolated "provincial town" on the river Kama, where he resumed his work on *Romeo and Juliet*. He visited Moscow in the winter of 1942 and then went back to the Kama, hoping to begin work on *Antony and Cleopatra*. By the middle of 1943 he was back in Peredelkino. As he told me, as a result of "the changes of the last three war years, the absences and the destruction, there was some loss and destruction of necessary books and papers. . . ." Incidentally, the town on the Kama strikes a familiar note. It sounds like the Quiet Mountains district where he had stayed in 1916 and which has provided some background for the Yuriatin chapters of *Doctor Zhivago*.

In the next two years I did not see Pasternak as often as I should have liked. He was hardly ever in Moscow, and I could not do the trek to Peredelkino so easily. However, I went there a number of times, and enjoyed the country air and the company. The train brings one to a country station, from which one has to walk a mile or so through rather mellow country of woods and open fields, a stream and, I think, a small river. Then one reaches the Writer's Village—some twenty cottages with small gardens all built fairly close to one another. This and the village proper are situated on the former estate of the Samarin family to whom Pasternak refers not only in his autobiography, but also in his poem, "The Old Park." Dmitry Samarin, a descendant of this family, had been Pasternak's university friend. He had philosophy and dialectics in his blood; and there are some grounds for thinking that he was the prototype of the "philosophical" Doctor Zhivago. I have already given a brief description of Peredelkino in my *Soviet Literature Today* (1946). The rural atmosphere of Peredelkino figures largely in Pasternak's poetry of the '40's and '50's; and in "Summer Day" he has really given us a portrait of himself engaged in gardening, a favorite occupation with him:

> "With us in springtime, until dawn,
> In orchards blazing bonfires flame—
> As pagan altars once had shone
> When fertility received acclaim . . .
>
> When toiling and in earth engrossed,
> My shirt I strip and throw away:
> With scorching sun my back's then glossed
> And baked like some big lump of clay. . . ."

That is very clearly Boris Pasternak as delving Adam. In a poem like "The Thrushes," also pervaded with this rural atmosphere, he is the lover of nature, meditation, and freedom.

But I have also been in Peredelkino in the winter which

can sometimes be grim according to the Pasternak of the war years:

> "A wintry kitchen. Petya's piping,
> A frozen room and blizzards' waste—
> All these may grow past daily bearing,
> And leave at last a bitter taste."

But I have been there when the winter sun made skiing very agreeable. I skied not with Pasternak, but with Zhenya Afinogenova, the widow of the dramatist. She died unexpectedly during a fire on board ship while returning from a visit to her family in Florida. She was a courageous woman who wrote a letter directly to Stalin protesting the persecution of her husband. She also had a *dacha* close to Pasternak's and I met him there too. I recall my last session with the poet, this time in his own *dacha*. I was about to leave for England, rather shaken by a long three year stay in Russia without any leave. We had a very prolonged, heart-to-heart talk covering many subjects. He again asked me to translate *The Last Summer (A Tale)*. He spoke of the past and the present, of his work and play. He dedicated several books to me. He showed me a drawerful of unpublished prose and spoke of "a more important work," by comparison with which his other works would appear "mere trifles." He asked me to look up his father in Oxford; but Leonid Pasternak unfortunately died a week or so after I arrived in London. However, I did go to Oxford and met Lydia Pasternak, the younger sister.

Pasternak also expounded to me some of his problems as a writer and explained how he was trying to adapt himself in an atmosphere of some misunderstanding to the general literary principles of Soviet Realism without sacrificing his art. But that was difficult because of the superficial level of literary criticism and little understanding for the problem of depth. In any case, he was now striving for greater naturalness and humanity. Like every soviet writer and intellectual, he was looking forward to being able to visit Europe after the war. He was very appreciative of the interest that had been shown his work in England.

The former student of Marburg University and the spiritual inhabitant of Shakespeare's London, seemed both familiarly and strangely rooted in this countryside, this Peredelkino, which he has imaginatively transformed and immortalized in his later poems. As his voice boomed on in long bursts of soliloquy, it seemed to range as far as Paris, London or the Urals. As he talked, Boris Pasternak seemed to fill the room. He then seemed to stretch out into the fields and woods beyond his cottage. Paradoxically he seemed to form a natural part of this landscape of pine, maple and birch. "Some sort of vegetable pondering was implanted in me," as he once said. But one felt in him too, as he once said about translating Shakespeare, that "there is room only for complete naturalness and full intellectual freedom. For the first I have prepared myself as best I could in the modest course of my personal work; for the second, I have been trained by my own convictions." In Boris Pasternak there is no grimace. No bitterness, no self-laceration. Instead, there is a spontaneous frankness and often a salutary silence.

III. THE POETRY OF BORIS PASTERNAK
(1914-60)

1. *Boris Pasternak as a Poet. General Development*

The fiftieth anniversary of Boris Pasternak's activity as a poet will fall in 1964. Since his debut with *A Twin in the Clouds*, his first book, we have to examine almost five decades of poetic development, five decades in which the poet has struggled not only to affirm his individual aesthetic, but also to purify it while, at the same time, striving to preserve his balance on the extremely slippery tightrope of revolutionary exigencies. In a turbulently galvanized Russia, Pasternak alone had the temerity to say in a public speech, "In an age of rapid tempos we must learn to think more slowly." He has practised what he preached and, by refusing to add to the meaningless flow of momentary rhetorical froth, has helped to contribute a more lasting monument to the expression of the human spirit. As a result, he has now suddenly emerged as a poet of both national and international stature and, in this morally crumbling age, he is also a man of character. He has also achieved what no other Soviet writer has been able to achieve: he has transcended both national and ideological barriers, and has addressed himself to the hearts and minds of men. Thus, he has reasserted the supremacy of the imagination. Naturally, there have been attempts to belittle him and even to label him old-fashioned, but the intrinsic quality of his work is too obvious, and his achievement too indisputable, to require any defence.

Boris Pasternak's poetry and his position as a Russian poet in the Soviet Union have a long and intricate history. Although he began publishing in 1914, it was only in the 1920's, under the Soviets, that he emerged into prominence. By 1934, after the death of Mayakovsky, he was generally recognized as a major poet, if not, indeed, the outstanding living poet of the Soviet Union, although Stalin had officially declared Mayakovsky to be "the best and most talented poet of the epoch." Pasternak is in no sense a type, but he is essentially a Soviet poet, because his poetic flowering (*My Sister, Life*) had coincided with the first years of the Revolution and because his further development was closely inter-related both positively and negatively with the Soviet scene. Whatever the Bolshevik diehards may say, he has lived there solidly or precariously for the last forty years and can therefore claim some share in the experience of his age and his generation.

When we consider Boris Pasternak's poetry from 1914 to 1960, it is clear that he has been, above all, a lyrical poet who has, in the end, preferred to accept and work within certain self-imposed restrictions of language, imagery and form, which derive in turn from a finally elected and deeply felt subject matter. He has a fine eye for detail, an intuitive grasp of unexpected conjunctions, and a masterly control of subtle rhythm. His poems give one the impression of having been inwardly composed and disciplined before they are committed to paper. The act of doing this may be compared to "a complete feeling that has burst into freedom." In this sense, freedom is the fulfilment of form; and it may also be likened to a ripened pear which must of necessity detach itself from the parent branch and suffer thereafter all the consequences of such an objective detachment.

The poetry, seen in perspective, also suggests that we must take into account various periods of development, major and minor. Pasternak's road has been long and rough. It stretches from his quick, boisterous and flashy debuts ("Had I but known what lay in store!" as he wrote in 1932) to the restrained and more deeply meditative tonalities of his later poetry. A whole world of varied and intense experience, a whole life of persistent questioning, a whole succession of illusions and disillusions, lies between *A Twin in the Clouds, My Sister, Life,* and the later *Poems of Yury Zhivago, A Rift in the Clouds.* But the note of savage despair, which characterized the earlier poems of Mayakovsky and the later work of Essenin, is strangely absent in Pasternak. On the contrary, a note of joy, ebullient or restrained, seems to pervade his work as a whole. This note could only correspond to a full acceptance of life and its consequences on a philosophical plane beyond that of mere social endeavor. The tenor of Pasternak's own personal life in adversity would seem to confirm this. His poetry therefore is the very opposite of pessimistic. This does not imply that he cannot be acutely critical as the occasion demands, whether it be in his *The Lofty Malady* or in a poem like *Wind* (i), or that he is not aware of all the personal and social problems when he writes ". . . it's harder to cut the pattern of my life/ than with a pair of scissors snip the water" (1932). But this note of joy or of love, so recurrent, consistent and reaffirming, which is often best expressed in an image drawn from nature as in the later poems—this note is dominant throughout; and this is what gained him the Nobel Prize. Joy is a feeling which Pasternak shares with Wordsworth, but Pasternak is more sophisticated, stricter and more objective than the author of *The Excursion*.

Pasternak's note of joy does not exclude the experience of sorrow. It also includes the mystery of life as resurrection, the mystery of self-renewing man and self-perpetuating nature. And, in this sense, Pasternak's poetry is one long continuous chant in celebration of the ritual of the Seasons and of man's dramatic appearances within their alternating but inescapable confines. Thus, Pasternak's theme, purified of its earlier verbal ornamentation and futuristic hyperbole, has become essentially a more austere theme—the ancient poetic theme of birth and flowering, decay and death. But within these four eternal walls, Pasternak, pitting himself against death, stresses the principle of rebirth and continuity, as he does in his poem *Bread* and various poems of the *Zhivago* cycle. (Joyce did the same in *Finnegans Wake*, but I am not suggesting any immediate connection between these two visions of life.) Actually the kernel of Pasternak's later vision is already contained in *My Sister, Life* as a whole and in one of its poems, *Epilogue 4*, in particular. As an integral part of his work, he pursued a theory of aesthetics which he has progressively elaborated and refined. As his Autobiography shows, he had moved away from some of his earlier aesthetic views, and his judgements both of his own previous work and that of some of his contemporaries had become austerely critical while he now extends his approbation to only a few finely sifted poets.

Thus, unlike Ulysses, Boris Pasternak in person has not travelled far and wide since 1914, but has rather cultivated his own garden. This seclusion was in the sense enforced, but he accepted it with philosophic calm. Here his own definition from *Safe Conduct* might apply: "The more

73

self-contained the individuality from which the life derives, the more collective, without any figurative speaking, is its story." The children of his imagination now travel instead. But in his garden up to the present many things have occurred: outbursts of lyricism, stops on the paths, attempts to grapple with snow and ice and the blizzards that blur the senses of direction, essays in narrative and conversation, flirtations with the epic, renewed song, longer halts, meditation, hours of re-examination and days of purification, time taken for translation, years spent on prose, and finally, after much assiduous labor, a return to lyrical poetry—a poetry more mature, rigorous and profound.

2. *Boris Pasternak as a Poet. The Early Period* (*1914-1923*)

> *"To love selflessly and unconditionally ... was the task of our hearts while we were children."*

To study a poet's chart is to follow more than a month of moons. A separate volume would be required to trace and analyze all of the poet's phases. For our convenience here, let me divide Boris Pasternak's poetic development into three periods: the early, the middle, and the late.

In general, over a bridge of some forty years, Pasternak's advance may be summed up as a slow and even laborious progression from a rich complexity to a richer simplicity. The dividing line came somewhere between 1932 and 1940. In his Autobiography, Pasternak now claims that he no longer likes the poetry he wrote before 1940, although he admits that "there are often grains of truth, aptness, and acute observation in the mass of what is deplorable and annoying about those things of mine." [1] It should, however, be realized that Pasternak has now also become criti-

[1] Boris Pasternak, *I Remember*. Page 121.

74

cal of the whole "modernist" period which helped to give birth to his early verse: "My ear was at the time perverted by the pretentious extravagances... that were in vogue in those days." [1]

In his youth, Pasternak capered and carolled, juggled with syllables, plucked images out of space, and made the hair crackle with verbs like sparkling combs, the ears vibrate with assonance and the teeth chatter with alliteration. The eye was keen, the command of language formidable, the associations surprising. The sensibility was fine, the impact of the rhythm infectious. It was an exciting new world of poetry: a poetry of exploration, of new verbal music; a poetry which had absorbed and which expressed many aspects of the modern ethos: a sense of relativity, a more dynamic tempo, a more fluid world. No translator can quite convey all the play of the dancing, sometimes harshly clashing, but always interweaving syllables.

"Lódka kolótitsya v sónnoy grúdi..." or "Róskoshj króshenoy romáshki v róssye..." These lines happen to be slow in movement, corresponding to the dreamy mood of this particular poem (*Oars at Rest*). Not all of his lines are so loaded with alliteration as the last one above. A more rapid tempo is given by the following quatrain from the poem, *Rain*, which is a frequent topic somehow symbolical of the poet's refreshing, watery world of frequent storm and shower.

"Oná so mnóy. Naigriváy,
Ley, smeýsya, súmrak rvi,
Topí, tekí epigrafom
K takóy kak tui, lyubvi!" [2]

[1] *I Remember*, page 105.
[2] Literally: She is with me. Play on,/ Pour, laugh, the twilight tear,/ Flood, flow in epigraph/ To such a love as you.

75

Certain of the more dynamic passages from Gerard Manley Hopkins suggest the early Pasternak in their alliterative rush. Here is a line from the *Leaden Echo*, translated into Russian, which reminds one of Pasternak: *"Otognatj, otpugnutj etikh slug i poslantzev..."* (*"No waving off of these most mournful messengers..."*) We should note in passing that Russian is both declined and conjugated, and this fact helps towards variety in rhyming. Pasternak often uses apocopated rhymes, and near rhymes between a noun and verb as, for example, *tomorrow* with *goes*, and he also uses the gerund form to rhyme with a noun (dusha: dyshav), a practise rather rare in Russian poetry until Pasternak's day. Pasternak's rhymes are accordingly often inexact or "ungrammatical." He has been criticized by the strict grammarians for this and also for some of his turns of speech, which have been adjudged "unRussian" i.e. not classically pure, but deriving from the South Russian dialect (Odessa), and also rhymes based on colloquial pronunciation. I would also note that the richest letter in Russian is *p*, just as *s* is the richest in English. Pasternak makes full play of the musical *p*s, but he also experiments with harsher letter sounds, the *k*s, *g*s and *zh*es, and this particularly in *My Sister, Life*. In a poem such as *Lines on Pushkin's "The Prophet"* the predominant consonantal sounds in the Russian text are *m, s, p, v, ch*. In the English translation (See Page 125), as the sense suggests, *s* is rather predominant, but in addition we have also *b, l, c, m, r* and *d* sounds. The sense often makes it impossible to keep to the same alliterative patterns. In the Russian translation of the Hopkins line, we note *t*'s, *p*'s, and *n*'s for the *f*'s and *m*'s in the original. Most of what we have just said applies in particular to Pasternak's third and fourth volumes, *My Sister, Life* and *Themes and Variations*.

His first two books, *A Twin in the Clouds* (1914) and *Above the Barriers* (1917) were a prelude to the more realized style of the two succeeding volumes. Pasternak reprinted only fourteen of the poems from *A Twin* in his *Collected Poems*—under the title of *Poems 1912-14*.

Though Pasternak now dismisses *A Twin in the Clouds* as a book with a pretentious title "in imitation of the cosmological ingenuities characteristic of the Symbolists...," [1] he had worked on those poems with great concentration in the summer of 1913. The book was a stepping stone from philosophy to poetry. As he says, "...for the first time in my life, I wrote poetry not as a rare exception, but often and continuously." [2] ... What was he trying to do in this first book? He claims he was trying "to avoid any romantic affectations," and was bent on introducing into his poems elements of interest for the reader apart from the main theme. He was not satisfied with the idea of a poem as a mere musical statement which could be easily declaimed. "I did not express, reflect, represent or depict anything at all." He stresses subject matter in another way. "My constant dream was that my poem itself should have something in it...a new idea or a new picture..." The poem should contain as fully as possible what he had set out to describe: one poem "to contain the city of Venice, and the other the Brest railway station." If this is true of the early Pasternak, it is also true of his later poetry, which is remarkable for its objective presentation of the thing described in itself, without the literary intrusion of either the ego or anything outside the object-in-itself. There would seem to be a link of continuity then between 1913 and 1940's. Similarly, the fourteen early poems also reveal

[1] Boris Pasternak, *I Remember*. Pages 76-77.
[2] Ditto. Page 76.

77

in embryo the theme of the Seasons, the first steps in that ritual dance. Nature is there, but the modern city is a very important element too. The modern city with its images of streets and railway stations rubs its stone and iron elbows against the softer contours of the images of nature. Likewise, the rush and rapid succession of unexpected associations, so characteristic of *My Sister, Life*, are already suggested in the opening stanza of this 1914 poem:

> "February now. Find ink weep!
> Go write of February in welling sobs,
> While slush rolls rumbling down the street
> And burns, pitch-black, with this black spring." [1]

The season and the month are there, but they are manifest amid the traffic of a city street.

Boris Pasternak, aged twenty-four, was no novice in the literary circles and salons of Moscow. At eighteen, he had already frequented the Symbolist circle concentrated round the Publishing House of Musaget. He had absorbed the novelty of Hamsun and Andrey Biely, Rilke and Verhaeren. He was very *au courant* of all the modern trends, French, German, Scandinavian, English and even American, to which Russia had been increasingly exposed since the 1890's. For the last decade translators had presented Whitman, Poe, Shelley, Ibsen, Verlaine, Kipling, and a dozen others. Modernism was in the air, aspiring to transform the world. The cultural revolution was battering at the doors of entrenched traditions. Ideas and styles succeeded one another with lightning rapidity. Groupings were both a vogue and a necessity. A battle was raging not only for individual positions, but also for the supremacy of ideas. The Russian scene reflected many of the European

[1] Boris Pasternak, *Collected Poems.* 2nd Ed., 1936. Page 217.

currents, giving them a specifically Russian coloration and intensity.

The Symbolist movement (Blok, Biely, Bryusov, Ivanov) had asserted itself aesthetically, philosophically and mystically before beginning to break up. In 1910, *Acmeism* (Gumilev, Akhmatova) emphasized craftsmanship. *Futurism* (Mayakovsky, Khlebnikov) rushed in noisily and militantly in 1912, proclaiming a dynamic future and death to the established idols, Pushkin or Blok. *Imagism* (Essenin), too, began to claim a following. These were the chief modernist *isms*. There were many more. Each of them faded away, leaving an imprint. They certainly enlivened the pre-1917 literary scene which, through death, had been vacated by all the 19th century giants. These *isms* were largely dominated by poets. Andrey Biely was perhaps the only prose writer who might be called the Russian contemporary of James Joyce because of his new concept of prose. Blok has named this period the "Spirit of Music," the uneasy movement of the masses which threatened to destroy culture and its rational forms.

In reality, the modernists were few in number. There were many writers of other persuasions: traditional realists, neo-realists, radicals, religious mystics. Bunin, Gorky, Korolenko, Andreyev, Alexey Tolstoy, Berdyaev. Writers like these had no particular sympathy for "modernism." As Gorky has said in one of his studies of Andreyev: "an attempt was made ... to understand it. But, on the whole, it was condemned ... There was no time to think seriously of literature: war and politics were of first importance. Blok, Biely and Bryusov appeared to be 'isolated provincials' or ... even traitors to 'the great traditions of the Russian commonwealth.' " [1]

[1] Maxim Gorky, *Lady Shura.*

In the midst of this intellectual free-for-all, Pasternak had begun by writing an essay on "Symbolism and Immortality," in which he had interpreted the Symbolism in a way that was to affect his own aesthetic.[1] By 1914, he felt attracted to the Futurists and especially to Mayakovsky. Mayakovsky had made a great impression upon him as a fated personality and a poet of unusual novelty and power. Mayakovsky, in the ascendant as a poet, was determined also to become a public figure in the teeth of all opposition. He injected his personality and his ego into what he wrote —a course fraught with dangerous consequences. He was also projecting himself into the political scene. Pasternak faced a dilemma. He did not want to compete with Mayakovsky on the public platform, either poetic or political. Nor was he prepared to involve himself romantically with the destiny of his poetry. He felt that he could fulfil himself only by pursuing the anti-romantic direction, without directly parading his ego in verse.

The European War and the Revolution did not immediately arrest any of the modernist trends in Russia, but they set in motion powerful new forces. By 1918, even the "rational" Maxim Gorky was appalled at the chaos. The day was rapidly approaching when the Russian intelligentsia would be caught between the Scylla of authoritarian Communism and the Charybdis of popular anarchy.

The war enabled Pasternak to spend almost two years in the Urals and there, removed from the Moscow literary scene, to perfect his aesthetic and work out his own idea of the poem. In *Above the Barriers*, there began to sound more clearly and more authoritatively the chief Pasternakian motifs, rhythms and tonalities which, when further developed in *My Sister, Life*, were to compel an army of

[1] Boris Pasternak, *I Remember*, pages 63-4.

poetical enthusiasts. In poems like *Petersburg, The Blizzard, The Urals, Spring, Three Variations, After Rain, Ballade,* and *Marburg,*[1] we are made aware not only of a wide range of new technical possibilities, but also of a distinctive poetic voice. The poet has succeeded in subduing his ego without smothering his personal voice. A variety of themes stand out: the city, nature, love, the poet and his definition of poetry, the seasons, the months, the days and the hours, the sunsets and the dawns, rain and snow reflecting mood and situation, flowering gardens and hard-paved streets. But, above all, these poems are informed by a dynamic musical movement.

The images of these poems of 1914-16 sometimes offer a parallel to the opening lines of *The Love Song of J. Alfred Prufrock* in the way they contrast nature and the modern city, where "the air is iron clamped to the night," "night rubbed against the elbow," and "the fears of the fallen walk." But, in the midst of the asphalt and cement, the telegraph poles and the motor cars, "the gardens have drained all this evening's shower." There is a note of joy in this line, but other images can suggest boredom or nostalgia, or the camps, battalions and artillery of war. There are fears or pressures, but Pasternak is never as desperately lonely as Mayakovsky. He is never the satirist. He has a lighter, more benign touch:

> "In days like these you lose your name,
> The crowds of people push you down.
> Your girl is with them too, remember,
> Yet you are never quite alone."

In contrast to Eliot, Pasternak's rhythmical pace in his pre-1940 poems is faster, more like that as if to satisfy the

[1] Boris Pasternak, *Collected Poems.* 2nd Ed., 1936.

insatiable demands of "greedy paper." The world of his vision has already been atomized. He snatches eagerly at the smallest concrete detail as if to save the world from complete disintegration. Thus in a poem,

> "The drowsy garden sprinkles beetles
> Like copper ash from chafing pans." [1]

In another poem, *Three Variations*, he suggests the vision behind his approach:

> "When to its very smallest detail
> The whole long day is weighed before you ..." [2]

These lines foreshadow his statement in *My Sister, Life* where, in *Epilogue 2*, he writes:

> "You ask who thus commands?—
> The all-powerful God of detail,
> The all-powerful God of love ..." [3]

Here we are almost in the garden of William Blake and his sense of the mystical importance of each blade of grass. Pasternak has never proclaimed himself as a mystic, nor has he ever used the word mysticism as far as I know. But there is much in his poetry to suggest that he has a highly developed perception for the microcosmic manifestations of life, nature and second-nature. It has poetry, both objects of nature and man-made objects often appear animated and autonomous. This is often true of his prose as well. Pasternak has a tendency to animate or personify inanimate objects and even abstract concepts, and to combine

[1] Boris Pasternak, *Collected Poems*, 2nd Ed., 1936, page 218.
[2] Ditto, page 258.
[3] See page 116 of this volume.

in subtle forms concrete and abstract notions as in "the smell of nettles, fungus, thatch, and fear ..." or in:

> "In August leaves, with asthma in each atom,
>   Dream only of quiet and the dark ..." [1]

Pasternak's method of breaking up the larger whole into minute parts, the "leaves" into their "atoms," for example, helps to make his poetry more elusive, mysteriously alive and surprising. It also makes it more difficult to follow, especially when accompanied by his verbal play upon the roots of words. His ardent pursuit of the word seems to draw him away from the sense, but he somehow manages to re-unite sound and sense in a chord within a dominant musical pattern.

Two additional observations may be made in connection with Pasternak's use of "detail." First, as Professor Roman Jakobson, now of Harvard, has pointed out in an essay,[2] *metonymy* is Pasternak's most frequent and characteristic device. When he writes "while slush rolls rumbling down the street," "slush" has assumed the attributes of a cart or carriage or car. And, second, I am tempted to discover the source of detail as part of his vision and aesthetic in a particular experience of his Marburg days. The vision, as distinct from the aesthetic application, seems to have come to him in the course of the experience he underwent after his proposal of marriage was rejected by the elder of the V. sisters. If we confront the *Marburg* poem with the relevant Marburg passage in *Safe Conduct*, we can hardly deny that the incident recorded in both these texts is of great poetic and aesthetic significance. In the poem, Pasternak,

[1] See page 121 of this volume.
[2] Roman Jakobson, *Randbemerkungen zur Prosa des Dichters Pasternak, Slavische Rundschau*, Berlin 1935.

after a sleepless night in Berlin, finally emerged into the street:

> "I walked into the square. I seemed
> Reborn. Each little detail lived,
> Imposing nothing, and then rose
> In every aspect of farewell." [1]

The external world, the world of the city and of nature, had suddenly become permeated, as with rain, with this newly awakened feeling, and had come alive in every minute detail. In *Safe Conduct*, he describes the experience thus: "I was surrounded by transformed objects. Something I had never before experienced crept into the substance of reality. Morning now knew me face to face and had appeared expressly in order to stay with me and *never* leave me ... Gradually the town began to stir. Carts, bicycles, wagons and trains began to glide in all directions. The fresh laconic quality of life was revealed to me. It crossed the street, took me by the hand and guided me along the sidewalk ... At some point in the future, I had to reimburse through work this morning's faith in me ... I was in every sense a new person ..." [2]

The influx of this new feeling may be compared to a manifestation of energy; and, as Pasternak says, he would build an aesthetic "on two concepts: the concept of *energy* (as feeling) and that of *symbol*." Hence "art is concerned with life when the ray of energy travels through it." Feeling, he argues, displaces reality. "Art is a transcript of this displacement. Art transcribes it from nature. How is nature displaced? Details gain in vividness what they lose in autonomous significance. Each detail has its substitute. Any one detail is precious. Any one picked at random may testify

[1] Boris Pasternak, *Above the Barriers, Collected Poems*, 1936, page 276.
[2] Boris Pasternak, *Safe Conduct*, Leningrad 1931, pages 52-53.

to the state pervading the whole of displaced reality." [1]
Instinctively, in a sort of daydream, an aesthetic had asserted itself.

This aesthetic, his encounters with Mayakovsky, his expanding range in *Above the Barriers*, and the necessity of further defining his own particular contribution, all these were elements that conspired to make *My Sister, Life* what it is—an extremely original and, I would say, refined or distilled cycle of fifty lyrical poems. Mayakovsky, however original in theme, form and language, was certainly not refined in either language or attitude; and he progressively sacrificed the lyricist in himself to the revolutionary propagandist. Pasternak, on the contrary, wished to preserve a certain balance by combining verbal and rhyming innovations, and a purely poetic theme, with a disciplined form. Pasternak's poetic history will show that he has preferred, with certain exceptions, to experiment with and play on variations within a definite frame, and that frame, in retrospect, appears to be the four-beat iambic quatrain. In this, he is nearer to Essenin and Blok than to Mayakovsky, whose free verse constructions seem more "modern." But this is the general picture. In reality, Pasternak offers great variety within his narrower framework: a variety of verbal orchestration, subtle modulation and intricate combination, as well as new sources of rhyme. Here is a transliterated quatrain, which suggests both a visual and auditory impression of the steppe:

"Kak byli tye výhody v tishj khor*oshy!*
Bezbrezhnaya stepj, *kak marina,*
Vzdikhayet kovyl, shurshat mu*rashy*
I plavayet plach *komarinyi.*" [2]

[1] Boris Pasternak, *Safe Conduct*, Leningrad 1931, page 59.
[2] See page 121 of this volume.

My Sister, Life, in particular, offers a variety of forms and metres, running the gamut from iambic pentameter quatrains to 4 and 3 and 2-beat iambic lines or variations on all of them. There are also some freer constructions as in *Finale*.[1] Nor is the *iamb* the only foot he uses. The *anapest* keeps turning up, as do the *dactyl*, the *amphibrach* and the *trochee;* and the latter two are sometimes used to vary the iambic feet.

The same applies to the sixty-four poems of his fourth volume, *Themes and Variations*, in which the difficult years of the Revolution make themselves felt despite their glad or sad gardens of love and the incessant chase after evanescent objects. The seasons, the months, the days and the hours are there. So are the vegetation and the showers, the lovers in parting or remembering. There is also sickness and blizzard, the snow-wrapped Kremlin and the crackle of rifles in the streets. There we find themes of joy, sorrow and nostalgia, purified by waves of rhythm. The poems, written mainly in 1918-19-21-22, prove that the poet had survived the hardest years.

3. *Boris Pasternak as a Poet. The Middle Period (1923-1936)*

"We are the music of the ice."

The Revolution had brought Pasternak back to Moscow. He arrived from the Urals with his new volume, *Above the Barriers*. Moscow was of course throbbing with political excitement. The days of terror were still remote. Literature, heated debates and utopian plans were still possible. The summer of 1917 was very fruitful for Pasternak: he wrote the poems of *My Sister, Life*, the key book of his early years. To publish it in 1918 or for some time after, was

[1] *My Sister, Life*, Berlin 1923, page 67.

a more difficult matter. It did not appear until 1922-23, and then only in Berlin. Mayakovsky, who had seen the manuscript in 1919 and liked it, had done his best, but in vain, to get it published. The same fate befell *Themes and Variations* (1923). These two volumes form the twin peaks of the poet's early period, but their public impact came after 1922. They were first reprinted in the Soviet Union in 1927, but some of their poems have been included in *Selected Poems* (1926). Until that date, no volume of Pasternak's poetry had actually appeared in the Soviet Union. Yet his reputation among Russian writers and critics in Berlin and Moscow had been firmly consolidated. He was often to become a butt for the warring schools of Marxist critics and, later, the Stalinist troubleshooters, but this did not affect either his poetic reputation or his appeal to an increasing circle of admirers. In fact, between 1926 and 1936, he enjoyed his best and most prolific period as a Soviet poet from the point of view of publication, circulation and public recognition.

If 1918-22 had been a period of survival, what followed was a period of adaptation. First, the NEP; and, then, the Five Year Plans. The problem was to adapt oneself to the rapidly changing scene of Soviet reality. Pasternak could not altogether isolate himself; to some extent, he had to join forces with Mayakovsky who was super-active and had put his Futurist cohorts at the service of the Revolution under the banner of *Lef*. In his speeches, Mayakovsky often mentioned Pasternak and defended him; he kept urging him to work in the *Lef* "laboratory." Mayakovsky was trying to establish *Lef* as the main center of Soviet revolutionary literary activity at the expense of other groups of writers, including the Communist and Proletarian ones. The 1920's were still a period of groups and rival discussions. Pasternak had a different idea of a poet's vocation, but he published some of his new poems in *Lef* and then in other magazines such as *Novy Mir*.

Apart from the lyrical verses of the *Miscellaneous Poems* (1922-28),[1] and some prose, Pasternak's main effort until 1930 was expended on four long narrative poems: *The Year 1905*, *Lieutenant Schmidt*, *The Lofty Malady* and *Spectorsky*. The first two are interconnected: they both deal with the events of the 1905 Revolution, of which the youthful Pasternak had been a witness. The poet was trying his hand at autobiographical and historical narrative in verse, but he brought to the narration his own rather complex, elusive, and dynamic style—a style not very suited to the longer poem. In subject matter, this was Pasternak's nearest approach to the ideological themes. These two poems came to be officially considered as his two most "revolutionary" efforts. But he was genuinely interested in the fictional reconstitution of his childhood years, and this too is his foundation as a novelist. These long poems are rather freer and more varied in form than either *The Lofty Malady* or *Spectorsky*. The latter poems are different in intention. *The Lofty Malady* is an attempt to grapple on a poetic plane with some of the realities, personal, social and political, of the post-1917 period. It contains critical comments and overtones, as well as an impressionist portrait of Lenin addressing the Ninth Party Congress. The poet and his circle are described as follows: "We were the music in the ice." Against a somber background the poet emerges as a figure with the eyes of conscience. *Spectorsky*, on the other hand, is a rather abstract atmospherical novel in verse of some 1300 lines told in pentameter quatrains. It is thematically related to the novella *The Last Summer*, and

[1] Included in the *Collected Poems*.

is autobiographical in character. It opens in 1924, but reminisces about the pasts as far back as 1913. The main characters are Spectorsky, a sort of contemporary Eugene Onegin, and two women, Olga and Maria Ilyina. The tone of the narrative is cryptic and often ironic. Spectorsky is the detached hero-observer of the troubled times.

By 1930, the year Mayakovsky committed suicide, Pasternak had reached a dead end in his poetry.[1] In fact, he was becoming increasingly interested in prose and the idea of a novel. He had just finished writing *Safe Conduct*, the publication of which would soon make him the object of critical and ideological attacks. In addition, he was about to become separated from his wife. But the upshot of it all was a reawakening of the lyrical vein in his poetry after a visit of discovery to Georgia and the romantic scenery of the Caucasus. The result was a new cycle of lyrical poems, *The Second Birth* (1932), of which *The Waves* formed a longish sequence of densely packed quatrains devoted to the imagery of the Caucasus and the shores of the Black Sea. There is a renewed lyrical intensity in these poems which had been lately missing from his work. There is splendid new imagery of sea, skies and mountains, and pertinent reflections on poetic and other problems. The style is terse, compact, and less involved. In *The Waves* we get our first clear premonition of the Pasternak-to-be, the champion of a new simplicity, when he writes:

> "Assured of kinship with all things,
> And with the future closely knit,
> We can't but fall—what heresy!—
> Into unbelieved simplicity."

[1] "During the last years of Mayakovsky's life, when all poetry had ceased to exist, either his or anybody else's..." —Boris Pasternak in *I Remember*, page 99.

The goal Pasternak had now set himself was not easy to attain. It took another twenty years to reach. In the intervening period, we are faced with many mysteries and changes in his situation. The wave of his publications continued till 1936. But we must note that he hardly published any new poems after *The Second Birth*, while many of his previous books were reprinted. As a sort of climax, two editions of his *Collected Poems* were printed in 1933 and 1936 respectively. *The Second Birth* forms the finale of both these editions.

But what was Pasternak doing after 1932? Apparently organizing a new domestic life for himself, writing prose, translating poems from the Georgian, appearing at Congresses and other writers' functions and, certainly by 1935-36 if not earlier, painfully working out a more restrained and realistic style for himself. In his Minsk speech in February, 1936, he made a clear reference to his poetic problem. "I shall be writing badly from the point of view of my past until ... I can adapt myself to the novelty of the themes and the propositions which I wish to touch upon ..." [1] These themes apparently required pondering and could not be presented in a brisk, light manner. In retrospect, Pasternak's early and middle poetry appears too musical, sparkling and rapid to support a weightier theme. The new, unspecified theme, evidently demanded a seasoned gravity. Did this imply a transition to an elegiac, an historical or even a tragic theme? Perhaps. The few poems of 1936, from *The Artist* cycle, are starker. They also seem to be concerned with the destiny of the artist in his day. This was certainly a new and far from easy theme on the eve of a new wave of Stalinist terror. But the ultimate result of Pasternak's protracted labor proved to be the

[1] See page 254 of this volume.

cycles of the *Zhivago* and *A Rift in the Clouds* poems, to say nothing of the novel itself.

4. *Boris Pasternak as a Poet. The Later Period (1940-1960)*

"Art is unthinkable without risk and the self-sacrifice of soul."

The Boris Pasternak of 1960 has survived the Purges of the thirties, the war, the Zhdanov Decrees, the anti-cosmopolitan drive, and the Nobel Prize furor. Let us first look at him on the threshold of the 1940's. At the First Congress of Soviet Writers in 1934, Pasternak had been described as "most remote from current affairs," "narrowly individual," "original," "infinitely far from trite," and "egocentric." [1] He was also officially and publicly summed up as: "Such is Boris Pasternak, one of the most remarkable masters of verse in our time—a poet who has not only gemmed his work with a whole string of lyrical pearls, but who has also given us a number of profoundly sincere revolutionary pieces." [2]

The Pasternak of 1936 was able to say publicly, *"Art is unthinkable without risk and the self-sacrifice of soul. We must attain in practice to the freedom and daring of the imagination . . . Do not expect directives in this matter . . ."* The Pasternak of 1937-38 was living in Peredelkino, almost in isolation, and in fear of arrest. The purges were on their way. He was no longer being published, but he was writing a novel and verse. By 1939, he seemed in the clear again, and some prose of his was published.

In 1943, during the war, *On Early Trains*, his first new book of verse since 1932, appeared. It was a slight volume. Most of the poems were written in Peredelkino in 1941.

---

[1] *Problems of Soviet Literature, Reports and Speeches at the First Soviet Writers' Congress*, Martin Lawrence Limited, London, page 236.
[2] The speaker was Bukharin, who was to be liquidated in 1938.

There was no mistaking the tone and the intonation, but something was different. There was less verbal play, a more serious tone, a simpler approach, an occasional elegiac note. Some variety in metre; no variety of form: the quatrain dominates and marches mostly on four-footed iambics. The general impression given by the tone and the flow of images and the rhythm was: less "foreign" and "modern," more traditional and Russian. I confess I was startled when I first read *On Early Trains* in 1944, and it took me some time to get used to the simpler vocabulary and the more transparent themes. Two years passed before I felt like translating any of the poems. What had happened to Pasternak? Perhaps he was in his Prospero rather than in his Ariel period. Perhaps, like the later W. B. Yeats or Alexander Blok, he had discarded an easier magic for a harder translucency.

The twenty-five poems of *On Early Trains* is a lean harvest after almost ten years of silence. Apart from the ten 1936 poems, the volume divides itself into ten poems written in early 1941 (the *Peredelkino* cycle), and five poems written later that year (*War Months*). We are struck at once by the fact that Pasternak, on the whole a city poet, has now become a nature poet as in *Summer Day* and *The Thrushes*. The country landscape of Peredelkino seems to have become an integral part of his vision, which has absorbed a variety of detailed country imagery. The Seasons, as in the autumnal *False Alarm*, figure here even more emphatically. But it is not only a question of the imagery; it is one, above all, of feeling and experience, too, of a slower, more meditative absorption in high philosophical themes, on the one hand, and a continuous visual observation of nature, on the other. This is not surprising, perhaps, if we remember that Pasternak had decided to live mainly in Peredelkino since 1937. The city is still a motif, but in a different sense from that in his early poems. The city (Moscow, of course, only twenty miles away) has become a more distant reality, something seen through a haze or an historical idea "like a ghost." [1] In the poems of *War Months*, we have Pasternak's more immediate reactions to the impact of the German invasion. These poems range from *Fearful Tale*, where the invader is seen, like Herod, slaughtering the innocent, to *Outcast*, in which Pasternak evokes his early impressions of the war, or to *The Old Park*, which provides him with an opportunity for an historical confrontation of the Russian past and present. The wounded soldier had a "slavophil" ancestor. The wounds "Are slowly being healed, assuaged..."

His next volume, *Spacious Earth* (1945), offers no further technical contribution or change except perhaps the thematic one of attempting to write on more topical and patriotic events as can be seen in the thirteen poems of the section entitled *War Verses*. The ten other poems are ninety per cent reprints of the *Peredelkino* cycle. The one addition here is a poem about Christmas, a nostalgic and visually vivid evocation of that festive and traditional occasion. It is written in stanzas of varying length and changing rhyming patterns, and in a combination of dactylic and trochaic metre. The *Zhivago* novel, as we know, is also full of almost ritualistic descriptions of traditional Russian occasions. The war poems, with one exception, follow the quatrain pattern. This exception, *At the River Mouths*, alternates a four-beat iambic line with a two-beat dactylic one. One of these poems, *A Fresco Come To Life*, which evokes rather curiously the siege of Stalingrad, is worth examining more closely from the point of view of its theme.

[1] See *The City*, pages 191-92 of this volume.

We must imagine a soldier in the thick of battle. In the first quatrain, embattled Stalingrad is realistically suggested. But, in the second, religious images are suddenly introduced: "The earth was humming like a prayer..." and "casting smoke as from a censer..." Among the ruins caused by the bombardment the soldier then begins to form an image, stimulated by childhood memory, or an old traditional world—that of "a monastery garden" and "a peasant commune." As a boy, the soldier also sees a fresco representing St. George. The poem ends on a triumphant note: The enemy is in flight and the future as reality holds out wondrous possibilities. As far as I know, this is the first mention by Pasternak of St. George, who was to become an important symbolic element in *Doctor Zhivago*. The religious tone and the imagery of the poem are also new, and they seem to foreshadow the atmosphere of the *Zhivago* cycle.

Fifteen years have elapsed since *Spacious Earth*. It is the last volume of Pasternak's verse to have appeared in the Soviet Union. This is indeed an extraordinary situation, which stimulates a lot of questions. But we must note that a number of his new poems, including *ten* from the *Zhivago* cycle, were published in various Soviet reviews up to and including 1957. To explain these phenomena, we must consider the background.

By the end of the war, Pasternak was enjoying a new wave of popularity. He was giving talks and readings in clubs, some of his poems were printed even in *Izvestia*, and a photograph of him had actually appeared in a newspaper. He had also become well known as a translator of Shakespeare. Until August 1946, it looked as if he had fully reestablished himself like Anna Akhmatova. But the national integration of the war years was short lived. The Hydra of ideology once more raised its violent head.

The Central Committee Resolution of August 14, 1946, and Zhdanov's *Report* upon it, pilloried a number of prominent authors past and present, including in particular Zoshchenko and Akhmatova, who were adjudged to be "persons alien to Soviet literature." Pasternak, though not the main target, was mentioned unfavorably. The authorities were now bent on imposing stricter ideology and eliminating "foreign" or Western influences. Individualism, "aesthetic subjectivism," and formalism, were all attacked and Socialist Realism was re-emphasized. The Resolution was soon followed by a number of diatribes directed against Pasternak. It inaugurates a period of some seven years during which no poetry or prose of Pasternak's was published. Nothing like these attacks had happened since 1931-32 or 1936-38. Fadeyev had succeeded Tikhonov as the Secretary of the Union of Soviet Writers, and he saw to it that no "decadent" matter should figure in the reviews. Literature was not the only field involved. All the arts were put through the mangle. This phase was still further complicated in 1948 by the "anti-Cosmopolitan" drive, which was also largely an anti-Jewish campaign. Continuing his life in Peredelkino, Pasternak was not too seriously affected by all this. He still had an income as a translator of Shakespeare and Goethe; and fewer public appearances gave him even more time to concentrate on his major project, which had become *Doctor Zhivago* and its cycle of poems (1954).

I shall not here go into the history of *Doctor Zhivago*. The cycle of twenty-four poems, which completes the novel, is an integral part of the whole conception and is supposed to reflect the inner poetical world of the Doctor and his experience of Calvary. The tone of the poems is deeply religious, philosophically historical, and "washed clean by suffering." Separation, suffering, death, and transfiguration are the themes within the historical framework of the Life of the Savior. The Seasons figure importantly as background motifs. The poems unfold like a slow, solemn ritual, one poem for every hour of the day. They point above all the theme of sacrifice, the necessity and inevitability of it when any great transformation is to be achieved through the word. Life has its joys, but it is still a path of thorns. Significantly, the cycle opens with *Hamlet*. Why Hamlet? The answer, I think, is given in the text, "*Hamlet is not a drama of weakness, but of duty and self-denial* ..." [1] Zhivago as a character is the very contrary of the ruthless positive hero, the terrestrial architect of human lives; he, like the artist, is involved in "the sacrifice of soul." How did Pasternak come to feel and express this deeply religious and symbolical theme? We do not know the full history, but undoubtedly the events of 1936-38, the irrational Stalinist blood bath, followed by the even more irrational blood bath of Hitler's *Walpurgisnacht*, had something to do with Pasternak's transformation and his openly manifested Christian tone, which testifies to a widening of his human horizons and a deepening of his inner convictions.

In tone, the Zhivago poems are grave; in vocabulary, deceptively simple and rich; in rhythm, solemnly sustained; in form, mostly sequences of quatrains—*Star of the Nativity* is the most varied and complex of the poems both from the point of view of stanza structure, rhythm and texture; in rhyme, subtle but conservative, more de-

[1] Boris Pasternak, *I Remember*, "Translating Shakespeare," pages 130-131.

pendent than hitherto on substantives and adjectives rather than on gerunds, adverbs and verbs. In metre, many poems in *iambics*, but also an unusually large number of them, almost half, in *trochees*, and some in a mixture of both; in texture, free from the interplay of sound effects; in music, chaster and relying more on the resonance of sense well turned than on sound unexpectedly achieving sense; in general, the effect of Bach rather than Scriabin. By comparison with the novel, more simple and direct; for the novel contains, perhaps, more elements linking it with the complexities of the early poems and the verbal and structural shifts of Andrey Biely.

Doctor Zhivago was rejected by the editors of *Novy Mir*, at the time of the post-Stalin "Thaw." While the novel was on its way to Italy, and while the storm of controversy was gradually beginning to break around him (the Soviet Press made some attacks in 1954), Pasternak had begun to write a new cycle of some forty-three poems, which we now know under the title of *A Rift in the Clouds* (*Kogda Razgulyatsya*). These poems were written in 1955-57. The title suggests a clearing up in the weather, a breaking of the ice, if you like, or a thaw. The title poem suggests a great movement of the clouds, the victory of sunlight. But, towards the end, the Pantheon of nature is transformed in the image of "stained glass" into an organ-pealing cathedral; and the final quatrain pictures the poet as a faithful and enduring acolyte in the eternal ritual of the world, the universe and nature. The mood is devotional and, in the end, ecstatic. The experience ultimately is both holy and happy.

This cycle may, therefore, be said to continue the devotional mood of Doctor Zhivago in his poems, but it is less obviously religious in its theme, since it lacks the clear

New Testament foundation and framework of the *Zhivago* cycle. In *A Rift in the Clouds*, Pasternak treats of a great variety of subjects, ranging from a statement of his aesthetics (*In Everything I Strive*), a discourse on Fame (*To be That Famous* ...), a lament on the mills of time and perished friends (*The Soul*), a visual and poetic conception of woman (*Eve*), to several snow scenes and a contemporary city picture of Moscow (*Bacchanalia*). Nature, the country landscape, the eternal forest, the Seasons, moments of realization or meditation in the poet's life, are all present in various admixtures. There are some poems reinterpreting and reaffirming Alexander Blok (*Wind*), who "has escaped all manufacture,/ And no one thrusts him down our throat." Here Pasternak stresses the fact that Blok's enduring greatness has not depended upon either academies or ideological bolstering. Much of what has been said about the *Zhivago* poems applies to *A Rift in the Clouds*. Here, Pasternak at times approaches the pure melody of folk song as in *The Soul*, for example. But, naturally, his is an artistic or sophisticated simplicity; and that is what he is striving for, judging by some of his statements in the *Autobiography* and by what Zhivago has to say on the subject in his diary in the novel.

Yet another cycle of poems is on the way. It was probably begun in 1958, and it runs through and sometimes reflects the troubled days of the post-Nobel Prize period. So far, I have come across and translated only ten of these poems. They are essentially an extension of the moods and themes of *A Rift in the Clouds* or, at least, they began in that way. How far the experience of the past year or more will bring about any change of mood or direction is not yet clear. The most recent cycle has so far followed the later pattern of form and style, which may be described as a striving for simplicity informed by the rich living quality of life.

("In everything I strive to reach / The very kernel: / In work and in exploring ways, / In pangs of heart.... / To verse I'd bring the breath of roses, / The breath of mint, / The scent of sedge, mown hay and meadows, / And peals of thunder...."—*pp. 201-02*).

The classical image of "the bow-string, tightly drawn, of a stubborn bow," with which the poem ends, contrasts with the images used in such definitions in the earlier poems. These had insisted on perpetual fluidity like that of water: ("Then, surely then, the stream can pour:/ And with blank paper under—rush!"—*p. 139*).

Boris Pasternak, as an artist, has come full circle. He even sits in judgment on his early self as in the Autobiography. Like a mythological serpent, he bites at his youthful extremities. This is natural. In his case, the old world was swept away. He feels that the early poetry had depended too much on the mood and history of a particular period. But "the support has been taken out from under that modern trend.... This striving, though true and original in its source, was not self-dependent enough to stand up to the trials of the changed years ..." [1] In our world, where continuity has been preserved, we can perhaps enjoy his earlier verse better than he himself can do now. It was an exciting world to create, and those compelling rhythms sang in many ears. "The most really contemporary poet of all my contemporaries.... You may like or dislike Pasternak, but you must believe in him." [2] In 1922, Tsvetayeva

[1] From a recent letter in English from Pasternak to Reavey.
[2] Sofia Parnok, "Pasternak and Others," *Russky Sovremennik* I, 1924.

had compared his poetry to a "luminous shower," and had called it "the poetry of eternal virility." [1]

In his late period, Pasternak is trying to realize more fully what he calls in a letter of his "the old, long standing, perpetually inherent urge toward the great and serious, towards the rapt and compressed." He is seeking a greater gravity and purity, something like "Pushkin's uncompromising clarity and Tolstoy's unwavering faithfulness to the facts." [2] Or again, "What I have come to like best in the whole of Russian litertaure is the childlike quality of Pushkin and Chekhov, their modest reticence . . ." [3] He is nearer now to the song-like simplicity of the best poems of Blok and Essenin. Indeed, he is striving to attain more nearly to what he has termed "nature's real ingredient or component . . . nature's own image or fancy of what she will grow or become . . ." [4] Boris Pasternak may now regret the years spent in silence or in translation—"I still have much to say, but life has come to its conclusion." [5] But let us hope that the years ahead will still be years of fulfilment. Already he has undoubtedly added further dimensions to both his poetry and prose: a deeper and more sustained emotional grasp of the subject; a sense of history and the place of art in it; a philosophical calm; a religious intuition; a rock-like conviction; a gift of focusing his energy to the desired end; and, finally, an understanding of realism which does not exclude the symbol as an essential part of our experience. Boris Pasternak is at present what he has always been—a lyrical poet, who has increased in stature and dimension, and who has respected his art by trying and sharpening his character.

---

[1] Marina Tsvetayeva, "The Luminous Shower," *Epopeia* 3, Berlin, 1922.
[2] Doctor Zhivago, page 195.
[3] Ditto. Page 285.
[4] From a letter.
[5] Ditto.

I.

My Sister Life
1917

To Lermontov

IN MEMORY OF *THE DEMON*

He came only at night,
In the glacier's most vivid light, from Tamara,
With his pair of wings pointing
Where must end or resound the nightmare.

He did not sob at, nor slander
The naked men, lashed and scarred on the frescoes.
And the tombstone survived
Behind the fence of the Georgian church.

Like a hunchbacked witch,
The shadow did not grimace under the grate.
By the lamp the *zurna*,
Barely breathing, did not inquire the Princess' fate.

But the sparkling tore through
The hair and, like phosphor, it crackled.
And the colossus failed
To hear the Caucasus greying for sorrow.

Some three feet from the window,
Sifting the woolen threads of burnous,
He swore by the ice of the peaks:
Sleep, my friend, I'll return with the avalanche.

THE DEMON—One of Lermontov's greatest works, an autobiographical
and romantic poem of the Caucasus.

Zurna—a type of primitive oboe.

NOSTALGIA

(It's Time for Birds To Sing 2)

For this volume as an epigraph
The deserts sound hoarse.
Lions roared and to a dawn of tigers
Kipling stretched.

Dried up, now gaped the ghastly well
Of yawned nostalgia;
And they swung gibbering and rubbing
Their chilled fur.

And then, continuing to swing in verse
Outside their grade,
They wandered in the haze through dewy lawns
And came in dream to Ganges.

The dawn, a venomed, famished viper,
Crawled into holes,
And jungles held moist air of requiem
And finer incense.

THE WEEPING GARDEN

(*It's Time for Birds To Sing* 5)

The awful one!—He drips and listens:
   Is he all alone in the world—
He crumples a branch like lace at the window—
   Or is there a witness here?

But clearly he chokes from the weight
   Of the oedemas—the earth is porous
And one can hear, far off, as in August,
   The midnight ripening in the fields.

No sound. And there is none to spy.
   Assuring himself that all's deserted,
He takes up his ancient tricks—he rolls
   From roof to gutter and spills over.

I'll raise it to my lips and listen:
   Am I alone in the world—
Prepared for desperate sobs if need be—
   Or is there a witness here?

All's hushed. Not a leaf stirs or rustles,
   No sign of darkness except a ghastly
Gulping and splashing of shuffling slippers
   And in between, sighs and tears.

DO NOT TOUCH

(The Book of the Steppe 3)

"Do not touch, the paint is fresh!"
    The soul paid no heed:
Memory's in stains of flesh—
    Calves, hands, lips and eyes.

More than all success or sorrow,
    For this I loved you,
That the light, now faded yellow,
    Flamed in you so white.

But I fear, my friend, my gloom
    Will whiter somehow
Gleam than lampshade, fever's bloom,
    Or white-bandaged brow.

PLAY RÔLE

(The Book of the Steppe 4)

O how you played and played that rôle!
And I, the prompter, quite forgot,
That you would sing another too,
Whoever tempted with the first.

Along the clouds a moving boat.
Along by meadows of mown fodder.
O how you played and played that rôle,
Like stern that cleaves a lapping sluice!

And fluttering at the helm quite low
Like a swallow with one folded wing,
You played it so!—Far better than
All rôles you played that rôle!

WITH OARS AT REST

(The Diversions of My Beloved 2)

In the drowsy breast the rocked boat is knocking;
Willows stoop down, my shoulders willows kissing,
My elbows and rowlocks their leaves caressing,
O wait and you also may have this blessing.

That's why this solace in song we find flowing,
For we know that's the ashgrey lilac blowing,
That's rosemary's dewy-crushed splendor glowing,
And lips and lips like stars for the claiming.

For that's to embrace the sky vault unending,
Throw arms round a Hercules huge unbending,
For ever and ever that's to be spending
Sleep on the thrill of a nightingale trilling.

STARS IN SUMMER

(The Diversions of My Beloved 5)

They whisper awful things,
Provide the right address.
Unfolding, they inquire,
And move as on a stage.

O silence—you're the best
Of all I've ever heard.
What torture for the rest
That mice have wings and fly.

The commons in July
Are wonderfully white.
Abysmal motives rule
The sky, and might cause harm.

They breathe felicity,
And radiance splash about,
At a precise degree
In the meridian placed.

The breeze tries hard to raise
A rose at the request
Of lips and hair and shoes,
Of hems and nicknames too.

They're gaseous, likewise warm:
In gravity they dip
All that was fiddled them,
All that for them was played.

ENGLISH LESSONS

(The Diversions of My Beloved 6)

When Desdemona was moved to sing,
And hardly any time remained for living,
Twas not of love, her star, she sang,
But willow, willow, sounded in her sobbing.

When Desdemona was moved to sing,
And strained her rising voice about black day,
For her the blackest demon there
Prepared a psalm of weeping river beds.

And when Ophelia was moved to sing,
And hardly any time remained for living,
All her parched soul was tossed and swept
As in a tempest stalks of straw are scattered.

And when Ophelia was moved to sing,
Too weary to bear the bitter fruit of dreams,
With what fine trophies did she sink?
With willow and celandine her bosom heaped.

Like shreds, from shoulders passion shrugging,
They entered, stopping in their hearts,
The universe—that pool immense,
In worlds to drench and daze their forms all loving.

OUR STORM

(Studies in Philosophy 5)

The storm as priest has burnt the lilac quite,
And dimmed with sacrificial smoke
Both eyes and clouds.—With lips you must requite
And heal an insect's twisted limb.

The clinking of the pails is knocked askew.
What greed: the sky will not suffice?!—
A hundred hearts keep beating in a ditch.
The storm as priest has burnt the lilac quite.

The meadow's all enamel. The blue had been
Scraped clean when all that ground was iced.
But even finches make no haste
To shake that diamond ecstasy from soul.

From tubs they still imbibe the freshening storm
By sipping from sweet caps of plenty,
And clover shows now purple and deep brown
In painters' splash of claret stains.

To raspberries mosquitoes fast are glued.
But the malaria-powered proboscis
Points here—the nasty brute!—its dart implanting
Where summer's splendor glows more rose!

To drop an abcess then right through a blouse
And, like red ballerina, leap?
To plunge its sting of mischief deep where blood
Like foliage, feels so damp and moist?!

Believe me, trust my game, and please believe
That migraine thunders in your wake!
Like wrathful day whose destiny's to burn
As wilding does on cherry bark.

So you believe me then? O slowly, yes,
So slowly, move your face more near, more close,
And in the radiance of your sacred summer,
I'll make it blaze, and fan its fire!

I shall not try to keep this fact from you:
You hide your lips in snow and jasmine.
I feel that snow so cooling on my lips.
Upon my lips it melts in dreams.

What shall I do with my abundant joy?
Put it in verse,
Joy's lips have grown so deadly dried and cracked
From poisons on the printed page.

A war with the alphabet they wage,
And on your cheeks in blushes blaze.

Pasternak's Note: These diversions came to an end when, departing,
she handed over her mission to her successor.

AT HOME

(*The Return 2*)

The heat hangs heavy on seven hills,
And doves strut in the mildewed hay.
From the sun the turban slips:
It's time to pull out a fresh towel
(In the bucket it's already dipped)
And wind it round the cupola.

In town there's a buzz of vocal chords.
Dolls and flowerbeds are shuffling.
We'd better sew up the curtains:
"With sulky mien he strolls and strides."
How soporific it is to live!
To kiss—what utter insomnia!

All soiled and grumbling—into bed
The city stumbles from the road.
Now for the first time from the steppe
There blows a breeze of sanity.
One can never drain
The stifling air of profanities.
Stars, posters and bridges—
To sleep!

Pasternak's note: From Paveletzky we departed that autumn too.

STORM, ETERNALLY FLEETING

(*To Helen 4*)

To a wayside station summer bade
Goodbye. And, doffing his cap, at night
A hundred blinding photographs
As souvenir the thunder took.

A lilac cluster dimmed to dusk.
Plucking meanwhile a bunch of lightnings,
He aimed with them to illuminate,
From fields, the present "Administration."

And when upon that building's roof
The wave of evil mockery did crash;
And when, like charcoal on a drawing,
The torrent crackled like a lash;

Then sunken consciousness began
To blink: and even those, it seemed,
Of reason's corners, which flashed light
As day, would soon be well-illumined.

EPILOGUE 2

*My friend, you ask me, who commands
That the idiot's speech be burnt?...*

Words slowly let us drop,
As gardens—peel and amber,
Unmindfully and largely,
Just so, and so, and so.

No need at all debate
Why ritually so
The foliage is besprinkled
With madder and with lemon.

Who made the needles tearful,
And poured across the stakes,
To notes, toward the shelf
Through a weir of jalousies?

Who daubed with rowan berry
On the rug behind the door
Those quivering italics
So gorgeously transparent?

You ask who thus commands
That August be so great,
For whom there are no trifles?
Who's engrossed in dressing

The maple tree in leaf;
And since Ecclesiast days
Has never left his post
At alabaster board?

You ask who thus commands
That the September lips
Of asters and far spaces
Should not be suffering so?

That the small leaf of broom
Down from gray caryatids
Might fall upon damp flags
In autumn hospitals?

You ask who thus commands?—
The all-powerful God of details,
The all-powerful God of love—
Yagailov and Yadvig.

Who knows if the riddle's answered
Of what's beyond the grave;
But life—like autumn silence—
Is always deep in detail.

Yagailov and Yadvig—primitive Eastern European gods.

And afterwards there was a hayloft,
Exhaling the smell of vinous cork
Since days when August had passed by
And paths were left unweeded.

On grass, on sorrel among the beads,
Clustered diamonds, frowning, hung,
Their very coolness to our taste
Reminding us of Riesling.

September was composing a statement
About the stableyard economy:
It flew and carried and instinctively
Gave notice of foul weather.

Now, pinning the yard, with red wine watered
It turned the sand and puddles yellow;
Now, from the sky it sprinkled lead
On half-round window frames.

Again, it gilded them and, gliding
From bush to croft, called on the peasants;
And now toward our glasses dashed,
Speeding from trees the fire of leaves.

Some signs of joy exist. Such words
As *vin gai, vin triste*, but please believe me,
That sorrel is nothing but a grass,
And Riesling a dusty term.

There was a night. There was of lips
The quiver. On temples, frowning, diamonds
Hung. In the brain a pattering of rain,
Which to my thought would not surrender.

It seemed, I did not love—but prayed
And did not kiss: and past
A mollusc swam, for neither age nor hour,
In glowing joy enshrouded.

Like music:—the eyes were all in tears,
But song dares not to weep,
Shaking, it did not burst in Ah!—
The soft and sodden coral.

EPILOGUE 4

To love—to walk, and still the thunder peals!—
To trample on nostalgia, wear no boots,
To startle adders, and with good repay
The evil done by cranberries and cobwebs.

To drink from branches whipping at the face,
Rebounding thrash the azure of the scars,
"So that's an echo!" and—finale then—
To lose one's way in plenitude of kisses.

As to a march, to stagger stuck with thistles.
To know by sundown that the sun's outlived
Those stars, those wagons laden with fresh oats,
That Margaret, that tavern woman too.

To lose one's tongue, subscription taken out
For storms of tears in the Valkyries' eyes,
And paralyzed, like this numb sky,
To melt the cross-beamed timber in the ether.

To clutch, while sprawling, in tuft and thorn
The years' events like prickly cones of fir;
The road; and then, descending, the Tavern's session;
The dawning day; we shivered; ate some fish.

Collapsing then, to sing: "With grizzled head,
I walked and helpless fell. The town was once
With bitter orach on the point of choking,
That swam immersed in eyes of soldiers' wives.

And in the shadow of long moonless barns,
As in the glow of oil lamps, grocery stores,
It's likely that he too—the aging man,
Will fall one day, while tramping, in his tracks."

Thus did I sing and almost died, and sang
And died again, and yet came back revived,
Returning to her arms, a boomerang,
And, if I well remember, bade farewell.

FINALE

Is this all real? Is it the time to run free?
Better to sleep eternally, sleep, sleep, sleep,
And shun all dreams.

Again—the street. Again—a canopy of tulle.
Again, each night—the steppe, a haystack and the moan,
Now and every day.

In August leaves, with asthma in each atom,
Dream only of quiet and the dark. A running dog then
Wakes the garden.

He waits till they go to bed. From the shadows
A giant, then another. Steps. "The door is bolted."
A whistle and a call: soho!

With our tread he literally drenched
And drowned the rough steppe road! With you
He racked the fence.

Autumn. Yellowish the doveblue skybeads lower.
Ah, like you, dank world, I'm wearied
Of this living death!

Untimely, night swings the censer
Of maneuvring locomotives: in rain each leaf
Strains, as they do, into the steppe.

The windows incite to scenes. How pointless!
The door heaves from its hinges, having kissed
Her elbow's ice.

Introduce me then to one who is sated
With the heavy wheat of southern harvests,
Wastelands and the rolling rye.

But one gets tired of being friends
With teeth on edge, with torpor, lumps
In the throat, and a plethora of words.

II.

Themes and Variations

1916-22

LINES ON PUSHKIN'S "THE PROPHET"

(*Variation 3*)

Stars were racing. Headlands seas embracing.
Salt was dazzling. And parching all the tears.
In bedrooms darkness brooded. And thoughts were racing.
The Sphinx to the Sahara turned its ears.

The candles sighed. It seemed as if, meanwhile,
The blood of the colossus huge congealed.
And lips swam wide in desert's azure smile.
With ebbing tide night evanescent reeled.

Gusts from Morocco stirred the sea. Simoom
Roared. Arkhangel snored in snows. Candles sighed.
The Prophet's lines, now roughly drafted, loomed
Just barely dry. And Ganges' dawn was nigh.

THE PROPHET by Pushkin is a famous lyrical poem based in technique
and subject matter on prophetic books of the Bible.

THE SICK MAN WATCHES

(*Sickness 1*)

The sick man watches. Six whole days
The snowstorms rage demoniacal,
Roll on the roofs in boisterous play,
Howl, prove their fury, till they fail.

The Christmas fades while blizzards blast.
He has a dream: They came and raised him.
He starts: "So it's my turn at last?"
(A summons. Bells.) Was it New Year?

Far in the Kremlin Ivan towers,
And, booming, swings, discarding caution.
He sleeps. The snowstorm is in power
Pacific, like that vasty ocean.

THE VOICE OF THE SOUL

(*Sickness 4*)

Scatter all things in the wardrobe,
And everything warm
Bundle together—sobs
Tear him to shreds.

Away! Do not waste labor.
If you hold on, I'll pull you out;
If you tear it, no great matter.
There'll be thread enough for patching.

Man! And no fear?
It can't be helped.
I am the soul. Rash
To the earthy end.

Does my benefit lie in braid
Or in a little dress perhaps?
Dared you suggest that, Man?
You'll pay dear for that.

Your eyes with wild thought
I shall amaze.
It is I have said it.
No, these are my words.

By that head of yours
I am taller than your sort,
I who have not been
And had never been.

THE PATIENT'S BLOUSE

(Sickness 5)

Of flannel, the wingless blouse of a patient
Conducts, like a penguin detached from the breast,
A longer, separate life from the body:
Move toward it a drop of heat or a lamp.

It remembers the skis. From harness and bodies,
Engulfed in the gloom, from shaftbows and girths,
Steam poured! We thought it was Christmas Eve sweating!
Our breath creaked whitely when walking or riding.

A house in the country and fear—nothing else:
And cupboards with crystal, and carpets and chests.
The house in its fever attracted the fence.
From outside, chandeliers with pleurisy flamed.

Devoured by sky, a wintry gleam in its eyes,
The bulging shrubbery bloomed as white as fear.
From the kitchen, past the sledge, a roaring oven
Spread women's huge kneading hands over the snow.

JANUARY 1919

(*Sickness* 7)

That year! How often by the window
He prompted me, the Old One: "Jump out, leave!"
The New has obliterated all
By recalling Dickens' *Christmas Eve*.

He whispered on: "Shake free, forget!"
And with the sun climbs in his stride,
Whereas strychnine that Old One brought
Or fell to flasks of cyanide.

With his own sundown, his two palms,
With his own lazily stirring hair,
He scoops—beyond the windows—calm
From birds, roofs and philosophers.

Indeed, he comes light-beamed, and lies
With panels and submissive snow:
He's heated, insolent, and cries
His claim to drink and shout his fill.

He is beside himself. He brings
The din of yards we must endure:
There's no nostalgia in the world
That snow will not completely cure.

BREAK

I

O angel a hundred times false, O immediately
I would pour a potion of purest distress!
But I dare not, or I claim a tooth for a tooth!
O affliction by falsehood begot from the start,
And, O sorrow and grief for this leprous condition.

O angel a hundred times false—it is not fatal,
This pain, this eczema, of the suffering heart!
By way of farewell, why a sickness of soul
So like to the skin's? Why so aimlessly kiss,
Like rain-drops? And why in public, like Time,
Mockingly murder for everyone's benefit?

2

O shame, you burden me! O conscience, in this break
So sudden, how many illusions still persist!
Were I a man—and not a mere collection here
Of lips and temples, eyes, hands, shoulders, fingers, cheeks!—

Then I'd let rip in crackling verse, in strident lines,
In the boisterous strength and freshness of nostalgia:
I'd have succumbed to them, and led them to the assault;
I would have stormed your citadel, my staggering shame!

3

If from you I cannot take my thought
At a party or over wine—in heaven then!
A neighbor, whom the bell to the hall has brought,
Will fling the door wide open to some man.

I burst upon them with December's air.
No sooner opened: "Here I am!" A corridor.
"You've come from there? What are they saying there?
What's new? What gossip in the town yonder?"

Is this fierce longing still in error?
And will it whisper later: "Cast in bronze?"
And from as high as forty feet prepared
To crash a question down: "That really you?"

Shall I be spared by public thoroughfares?
Ah, if you knew how fiercely longing seizes
When streets a hundred times a day now stare
At me, suggesting you in false resemblance.

4

Come, try and impede me. Attempt now to smother
This mounting nostalgia that crackles today
Like mercury in the void of Torricelli.
O obsession, prohibit—impede me and hinder!
Prevent me from raving about you! Be shameless: we are
    alone.
O smother, smother!—More fiercely.

5

Weave this shower, like waves, of cold elbows,
And, like lilies, of powerless palms, satin and strong!
Break away, exult! Into the open! O catch them! For, in
    this furious chase,
There is the clamour of woods choked with the echo of
    hunts in Calydon,

Where, like a roe, Actaeon heedless pursued Atalanta
    towards the glade,
Where they loved in fathomless azure whistling by the ears
    of the horses,
And kissed in the impetuous baying of the chase,
And caressed in the peals of the horn, the crackling of trees,
    hooves and claws.
Oh, into the open! Into the open!—Like those!

6

You're disillusioned? Thought we'd better part,
This world in requiem of swan-song leave?
On grief relying, her pupils widening large
And tear-bedewed, invincible would prove?

At mass, the frescoes crumble from the vaults,
Loosened by contortions of Sebastian's lips;
But, as from now, my hate perceives the fault—
Delay, and I regret the urgent whip.

Recovering quick, without least thought or pause,
She now resolves to plough up all the rest.
Like—Time. For suicide she finds no cause,
And thinks it slow—a tortoise at the best.

7

My friend so tender, O precisely as at night, when flying
    from Bergen to the Pole,
By the warm down, like tumbling snow, cascading from
    the legs of grebes,
I swear, my tender soul, my dear, I swear, it's not against
    the grain!
When I admonish you: forget, and fall asleep, my friend;

When like a stiff Norwegian breaker to its funnels jammed
    with ice,
Within the sight of winters and those motionless frosted
    masts,
I, like a fool, rush in the commotion of your eyes: sleep,
    find comfort,
It will heal before the wedding, my friend; be consoled,
    and do not weep.

When northward quite beyond the ultimate habitation,
By stealth from the arctic and ever wakeful icebergs,
While a midnight cupola rinses the eyes of blinded seals,
I urge you still: rub not your eyes, sleep and forget—it was
    a trifle.

8

This table is not broad enough to bear my chest
Upon its board or beyond the brink of anguish
To crook my elbow or just past that isthmus
Of so many miles of freshly ploughed Forgive.

There, now it's night—behind your sultry hair,
They've gone to sleep—behind your shoulders' realms,
They douse the lights—but I'd bring them back at dawn,
And this porch would brush them with a drowsy branch.

With hands, not snowflakes on them! They suffice!
O torment's fingers ten, with the blanching furrow
Of Twelfth-night stars, like semaphores that signal
The trains delayed that rolled through blizzards North!

9

The shuddering piano flicks the foam from lips.
This fever sweeps and scythes you off your feet:
You say, "My dear, my darling!" But I cry,
"No, no! While music's playing?! How could we meet

In twilight closer than we are, with chords—
An avalanche of diary sheets tossed yearly
Into the fire?" O wondrous understanding, nod,
Nod approval, be amazed!—For you are free.

I'll not detain you. Go, be generous breath.
Go, join the others. Enough of Werther's pains.
For in these days the very air reeks death.
An opened window is an open vein.

WE WERE FEW

(*I Could Forget Them 4*)

We were few. Perhaps only three.
From the Don, hellish and burning,
Now beneath the grey-scudding bark
Of the rains and the clouds and soldiers'
Soviets, verses, and all the debates
About problems of transport and art.

We were people. But now we are epochs.
We were shaken and are caravan-sped,
Like the tundra to sighs of the tender
And the panting of pistons and rails.
Flocked together, we'll irrupt and touch,
Then swirl in a whirlwind of ravens,

And—past! You'll understand when too late.
Thus striking heaped straw in the morning—
Instantly tossed in confusion—
The wind chatters thereafter forever
In the trees' storm-conducted assembly
Raging above the ragged thatch of the roofs.

WHEN SLANTING FRAMES

(l Could Forget Them 5)

When slanting frames in rhythm shower
And break in time from hook and wall
As gusty road makes my candle cower
I cannot teach them not to fall.

What if the universe wear a mask?
What if there be no space so wide
Whose mouth with putty they do not ask
To stop when they have so decided?

When there is reason for the shower,
When things in song have cause to rise,
They shed authority, drop honor,
And finally throw off their guise.

SPRING

(*Unsad Garden 12*)

Spring! I am from the street where the poplars stand
    astonished,
Where the distance shies in fright, where houses fear to fall,
Where the air is blue-washed, like the linen bundle
Of a patient just discharged from a hospital.

Where the evening is vacant, like an interrupted story,
Ending in asterisks without any sequel
To the suspense of a thousand clamoring eyes,
Bereft of expression and deeply abysmal.

  Asterisks are sometimes employed by Continental printers where
American printers would use a line of dots.

EVERY DAY

(*Unsad Garden 18*)

Every day, from ten till two,
The garden gasped the sultry air
Of snakes, ozone and rosemary,
Made oleanders dully stare.

The whitewashed attic glimmers blue;
The farmstead drowses; nobody intrudes;
A grey-hued raspberry bush, and yonder
The lilac background of its preludes.

At whom a baby adder hisses?
To whom a rosebush waves farewell?
Summoned, Chopin again addresses
His soul to a ballade's plaintive spell.

When we lack means to cure or heal her,
Diphtheria spreads her summer brood.
Black sources! Shall we now or later
Unlock for her the gushing blood?

To touch her hand—that's all we must
To quarantine half of the world;
And where plantations raise their dust,
Tobacco plants breathe parching mold.

POETRY

(*Unsad Garden 22*)

Poetry, on you I'll stake my oath
And finally end up by gasping:
You're not the pose of sugared kind;
You're summer in a third-class carriage;
You're suburbs rather than refrain.

You're stifling Yamskoy street in May;
Shevardin's battle-bastioned night,
Above which clouds exhale deep groans
And, breaking ranks, go several ways.

And doubled by the winding track—
A suburb rather than refrain—
Men crawl from stations to their homes,
Not raising song but stupefied.

The shower's shoots are soiled in clusters,
And until dawn—longtime, longtime,
They drip acrostics from the roofing
And rouse the bubbles into rhyme.

Poetry, when under a faucet's stream
A truism gapes like a tinny pail,
Then, surely then, the stream can pour:
And with blank paper under—rush!

Note: Shevardin's defence of this bastion is mentioned in *War and Peace*.

III.

1905

1925-26

CHILDHOOD

(*1905—Part 2*)

I was only fourteen.
The *Vhutemas* now here established
Was still a school of sculpture then.
Upstairs,
In the wing where the Workers' Faculty is now,
My father had his studio.
Our apartment
Was a quarter of a mile away
Where a century of dust
Lay on Diana and the canvasses.
Flagstones on the floor,
And on the flags a spatter of mud.
Those were the winter's mazes.
Port Arthur had surrendered,
But cruisers steamed to the Pacific.
Armies had been dispatched;
Squadrons were expected;
The twilight,
The colors of a palette
And the professors—
All these stared at the old central Post Office.

What a variety of types and faces!
Here's a psychiatric case.
Here, a blockhead.
And, there, someone sensitive and warm.
Here, again, a perfect puppy.
The classrooms too full for an apple to fall.
And the hothouse heat.

Vhutemas—a school of applied art.

The bells at Saint Flaurus-and-Laurus'
Blended with the shuffling feet.

One day,
When the fracas behind the wall,
Like the tide, did not die,
And the whirlpool of rooms was immovably tall
And the street with gas was alive—
The doorbell rang
And the sound of voices drew near:
Scriabin—it was he.
Oh where could I run
From the footsteps of my divinity!

The holidays caught up.
Quarterly reports.
The semester's end.
With strings sparkling
The grand stood open
Day and night.
There was even time to compose
In the morning and all day long.
Days moved on.
Christmas was running out.
We gave so much to Christmas trees!
If we could only get a little back.

A Petersburg night.
The air, like a black iceberg, swells
From needle steps.
No one obstructs.
Some wore overcoats, others a sheepskin coat.
Like a silver coin, the moon grew chill.

Something's up in the Narva quarter.
The crowd roared:
Gapon.

A hum in the hall.
A stifling atmosphere.
The trees had counted about five thousand.
Into hallways drifting from the street,
The snow makes moldings on the stairs.
Here's the maternity clinic.
And in the unfrescoed vaulted womb,
Thrashing against the walls of rooms
Like a raw lump—
This century.

A notorious dawn.
The clouds very close and with cranberry stuffed.
We heard galleries creaking,
And the breath of slops curled like smoke.
People, dashing out, walked
From gallery to gateway,
Under gonfalons
From the gateways—into the frost,
Into the free space
Kindled by winter.
Eight thundering waves
And the ninth,
Grandiose as the horizon.
The caps were washed away from heads.
O Lord, have mercy on thy people.
To the left, a bridge and a ditch.

Gapon—the priest who led the demonstrators to the Winter Palace on
Bloody Sunday, January 9, 1906.

To the right, a cemetery and a gate;
A wood behind;
And ahead a railway track.
On the Kamenno-Ostrovsky
The pavements stand on stilts,
Gaping from flowerbeads and kiosks.
Behind the procession splashes the tail
Of those who had broken the lock
Of the crossroads
And the pouring streets.
The demonstrators had reached the park.
They begin crossing Trinity bridge.
Eight salvos from the side of the Neva.
And the ninth
As weary as glory.
That's—
(From left and right, the trotting cavalry.)
That's—
(The horizons yell:
We'll get even yet for this massacre.)
Those are the joints being torn
Of the Dynasty's oaths
Of loyalty.
The sidewalks were full of people running.
Dusk fell.
The day cannot rise.
To the drumming of salvos
The barricades reply with shots.
I was fourteen years of age.
In a month I'll be fifteen.
These days were like a diary.
One read them at a guess.
At any page.

We played at snowballs.
We kneaded them from the units falling
From the sky,
From flakes and arguments that marked our day.
This landslide of reigns,
This drunken downpour of snow:
This was the courtyard of the *Gymnasium*
On the corner of Povarsky street
In January.

Not a day but a blizzard.
Our seniors—
Those in the Party especially—
Had the look of eagles.
But we juniors:
Unpunished, we were rude to our Greek master,
We stacked our desks against the wall,
We played at parliament in class,
And in fancy roamed
In the underground with Georgians on the run.

For the third day snow had fallen.
It was still falling in the evening.
During the night
The weather cleared.
In the morning—
A thundering peal from the Kremlin:
The patron of the Arts School . . .
Sergey Alexandrovich . . .
Killed . . .
In these early days of February,
I fell in love with the storm.

IV.

The Lofty Malady

1923-28

THE LOFTY MALADY

The moving rebus flashes by
The siege is on, the days move on,
The months and years all pass away.
Then one fine day, the pickets
Stumbling in their haste,
Bring news: the fortress yielded.
They don't believe; believing, light the fires,
Blow up the vaults, seek the way in,
Come out, go in—the days move on,
The months and years all pass away.
Years pass away—and all is in shadow.
Then epic Troy is born.
They don't believe; believing, they light fires,
Impatiently await the martial measure;
They weaken, lose their sight—the days move on,
And the vaults of fortress crumble.

I am ashamed, and every day my shame increases,
That in an age that casts such shadows
A certain lofty malady
Still bears the name of song.
Is Bedlam a fitting name for song,
A lesson earth has learnt
The hard way, turning from books
To throw itself on pikes and bayonets.
Hell is paved with good intentions
There's an accepted point of view
That, if we pave our verse with them,
All trespasses will be forgiven.
All this shocks the ears of silence.

Those who returned from war
Have learnt in days of ruin
How taut our hearing's strung.

In those days we all conceived a passion
For storytelling, and winter through the nights
Grew never tired of twitching from the lice,
As horses twitch their ears.
Those were the ears of brooding darkness
Stirring, wrapped in fallen snow,
And we in tales were turning
Upon peppermint cakes of pillows.

In spring a trembling overcomes
The upholstery of theater boxes.
And February, in want, is most untidy.
He'd groan at times, and cough up blood,
And spit; then quietly go off
To whisper in the ear of freight cars
Of this and that, the track, the rails,
About the thaw and anything at all;
Of soldiers from the Front on foot.
And you're asleep, expecting death,
While the narrator doesn't give a damn:
The wardrobe louse, that never tires
Of pricking up its ears, will swallow
Truth and falsehood all entangled
In jugs of water-logged galoshes.

Although at dawn the hardy thistle,
Persisting to cast the longest shadow,
Tried to prolong the morning hours;

Though, as of yore, the country road
Would arrest the wheels in shifting sand
And rush them out again to firmer soil
Where stakes and landmarks reassured;
Although the autumn vault, as now,
Was clouded, and the forest gazed from far,
And evening in the haze was chill;
Yet, this was plainly forgery,
And sleeping earth, caught unawares,
Resembled a small child's convulsions
Or death or cemeteries' silence,
Or that extraordinary hush,
Which sleepingly enfolds a district,
And, shuddering every now and then,
Struggles to remember: "Tell me now,
What was I trying then to say?"
Although the ceiling, as before,
In serving to support a cage,
Had dragged the second floor to third,
And hoisted the fifth up to the sixth,
Suggesting by this change what is:
That everything is still the same;
Yet plainly this was forgery;
And through the waterpipes' system
There mounted to the top that empty,
Breath-sucking scream of troubled times,
The stench that reeks of burning newspaper,
Of laurel and some Chinese suey,
Which was more irksome than this verse,
And, rearing a mile into the air,
Did seem to grunt: "I say there, wait;
Was there something I did want to eat?"

And like a hungry tapeworm crawled
From second floor up to the third,
And then crept on from fifth to sixth.
It exalted hardness and stagnation,
But tenderness declared illegal.
What could we do? The sound vanished
Behind the rumbling of increasing skies.
Their noise, alighting in a station,
Was fading behind the water tower,
And they were borne beyond the forest,
Where the embankments looked like a rash,
Where mid the pines, much like a pump,
A snowdrift, rocking, wildly rocked,
Where rails went blind and scratched themselves,
And barely touched the swirling blizzard.

But there behind, in blaze of legends,
The hero, intellectual, and fool,
In fire of slogans and decrees,
Burnt to the glory of the dark power
Which, surreptitiously in corners
Ironically mocked, defamed him
For his achievement, or if two
And two did not add up a hundred.
But there behind, in blaze of legends
The intellectual-idealist
Continued to print and pen his posters
About the joy of his decline.

In sheepskin swathed, the bonded serf
Stared back where north was falling dark,
And snow for all its worth competed
And strained with dusk-imposing death.
Like an organ there, in mirrors' ice,

A station glittered enigmatic,
Forebore to close its eyes, groaned grief,
And in wild beauty quarrelled with
The Conservatory's void
In time of holidays and repairs.
Unbearably, enfeebling typhus,
Having now embraced our knees,
Dreamt on and on and shuddering heard
The motionlessly gushing motif
Of crumbling self-abasement.
He knew the range of organ flutings
And collected with the dust in seams
Of the bellows' folded shirts.
His ears, so highly critical,
Entreated still the thickened dark,
The ice and puddles on the floor,
To keep their silence very dry.

We were the music in the ice.
I speak of those in my own circle,
With whom I had it on my mind
To leave the stage, which yet I'll do.
Here shame can have no place.
I was not born to look three times
In different ways into men's eyes.
Far more ambiguous than song,
The dull, blunt word of "enemy."
I'm guest.—To guest in all the worlds
Is lofty malady.
All life I wished to be like all,
But, in its beauty, this our age
Proves stronger than my whimper
And desires to be like me.

We were the music of the cups,
Those gone to sip their tea in dark
Of forests dense, oblique behavior,
And mysteries that flatter none.
The frost was crackling, and buckets hung.
The daws were circling; the deep-chilled year
Was thoroughly ashamed of gateways.
We were the music of ideas,
Preserving way to the outside
But, in this chill, to ice transforming
The slushy damp of the back door.
But I witnessed the Ninth Congress of
The Soviets. In the damp of twilight,
Having run before to twenty places,
I cursed both life and cobbled roadways;
But then next day, as I recall,
The very day of celebration,
I strode excited with a pass
To the theater and the stalls.
I went quite soberly on sober rails,
Stared around while the surroundings looked
Completely gutted and laid waste,
Refusing flatly to recover
Or even rise from their deep rut.
From papers posted on the wall,
The Karelian problem stared
Eliciting a question
In rather sickly big-eyed birch trees.
On telegraph supports, the snow
Was settling down like a thick braid,
And winter day on branches' canvas
Drew to a close as was its custom,
Not of its own accord, but in reply

To an instruction. At that moment
The moral of that faery canvas
Seemed contained in *The Convention*.
That genius' exalted fever
Proves whiter and stronger than cement.
(Who did not help to push that barrow
Had better suffer, bear his sickness.)
How suddenly at the week's end
The creator's failing eyes might vision
A great stronghold's ramparts rise
Or just a teeny-weeny little fort.

Novelty nurtures successive ages;
But its impressive golden pie,
The while tradition stirs the sauce,
Sticks in our throat and makes us choke.
Now, at some distance and remove,
Mean trifles grow invisible.
The stereotype of speeches is forgot,
For time has evened out the details
Where trifles have predominated.

The farce for me is not prescribed
As medicine against all trials.
Nor do I now recall the basis
For my recording a glib vote.
I'm now oblivious of the day
When, in the deep Pacific depths
Of gaping Japanese abyss,
A telegram could tell the class
(What an erudite sea-diver!)
Of workers from the class of octopi.
And when those fire-exhaling mountains

Seemed to lie outside its judgement.
But many things are far more stupid
Than to classify Pompeii.
I long remembered well by rote
The blasphemous wire then dispatched!
We sent the victims of the drama,
To smooth the horror of Fujiyama,
A routine Trade Union agit-print.

Awake, O poet, show your permit.
Here it doesn't do to yawn.
Into the pit from boxes rush
Msta, Ladoga, Sheksna, Lovach.
Again from the Assembly Hall,
In the doorway opening full South,
There blew across the lamps the fanning
Breath of Petrine arctic blizzards.
Again the frigate went broadside.
Again a forceful billow gulping,
The child of treachery and wile
Admits no more his native land.
All's drowsed by night when, halloing loudly,
Beneath the Imperial train till dawn
Through all the region of the coast
The hunters' packs have scattered over ice.
The clink of spurs went hunched.
Tradition hid its formal stature
Behind the body of the railway,
Beneath the bulk of railway bridge.
Two-headed eagles now were veiled,
And in the darkness Pullman cars
For hours rested in fields,
And it smelled of March upon the earth.

By Porhovo, in wet tarpaulin
Of waters billowing for miles,
A munitions factory awoke
And through the Baltic region yawned.
And the two-headed eagle tired,
Circling over the lands of Pskov,
Of the beaters' tightening the ring
Of the anonymous rebellion.
Ah, if they could but find the track
That's unrecorded on the maps.
But the supply of sleepers marked
On maps was dwindling rapidly.
All they could do was try again
The exhausted tracks of permanent way.
Nearby, streams played close to the track;
The future turbidly looked dim.
The circle narrowed, pine trees rarer grew,
Two suns in windows met each other.
One sun was rising out by Tosna;
The other was sinking in Lower Depths.

How shall I end my fragment now?
As I remember, the accents of
His voice struck sparks from off my hair,
Like crackling lightning when it spins.
The audience rose, with eyes in vain
Examining the farthest table,
When suddenly he grew up on the tribune,
And grew up there before he entered.
Then imperceptibly he slipped
Right through the row of obstacles
And prompts, like a storm materialized
That bursts into a smokeless room.

Then the roar of ovation broke,
Like the release, like shell's explosion,
Having no power but to explode
In the ring of barriers and props.
And he began to talk.
That we remember, and we honor
The monuments to those that fell.
I speak of fleeting things. Of what
In him was instantly particular.

He was like a rapier's sudden lunge.
Pursuing what has been pronounced,
He pressed his point, his coat awry,
Fixing the uppers of his shoes.
He might have been discussing oil,
But his body's animated line
Breathed the bare kernel of the thing
Which had burst through the stupid husk.
And his so strictly guttural words
Were quite vociferous in all
Relating to the blood of fables:
He was their sound personified.
When he referred to plainest facts,
He knew that, rinsing out their mouth
With his own vocal extract, through them
In person history was bawling.
And feeling freer than with others,
And always ready to carp at it,
He only with history was curt.
With ages' envy envious,
And jealous with their jealousy,
He ruled the current of ideas
And, in this way, the country too.

V.

The Second Birth

1932

THE WAVES

I

Here all things meet: all I have lived,
And all that guides me still through life,
My aspirations and foundations,
And what I witnessed with my eyes.

The sea confronts me, waves unfurling.
The waves are many. Their count infinity.
They teem. They sound in minor key.
The surf is baking them like waffles.

As by a herd the shore's bespattered.
They teem as though the sky expelled them.
He's loosed the herd to pasture freely,
And sprawls, himself, behind a hill.

Herd-like, and furling into funnels,
Where my nostalgia browses widely,
My acts come running now to me—
The crests of all I have experienced.

They teem. They have no count, no sum;
Their sense as yet is incomplete;
But with their change all things are garbed,
Like singing sea with spray of waves . . .

Waffles—the word in the original, translated as "waffles" [*vaffli*], is obviously a loan-word from English and can really be translated by no other term.

Here mountains will be seen at rest:
Illusion of hush: the roar in a gully;
Their stillness now: the sheer, restrained
Excitement of first rendezvous.

Dawn glimmered. Beyond Vladikavkaz
A shape bulked black. And ponderously
Clouds moved. The dawn came not at once.
It glimmered, but the light delayed.

For three miles round the weight was felt
Of darkness shrouding all the peaks,
Though, gathering courage, some of them
Attempted to throw off their yoke,

From there a sort of sleep was wafted.
Like a pot fixed firmly in a stove,
Dagestan was simmering, pent inside—
A dish of poison in a pot.

He rolled his peaks toward us
And, black from head to heel,
Seemed eager to receive the car
Not at dagger's point, but in the rain.

In mountains porridge was stirred up.
One giant's bigger than another.
Each fiercer, handsomer than next,
Barred in the exit from the valleys . . .

Here all things meet: all that I've lived
In foresight and in waking dream,
All those whose worth I am below,
And that which gave me some repute.

In these categories' turmoil
The foremost place in couplet goes
To forests of the Adjar foothills
By the sea shore of white Kobulet.

So you're still here, and I've been told
Where you are now, and where at five.
I could have found you in the Kursaal
Instead of letting my tongue wag.

You would have listened and grown younger,
A woman adult and self-possessed,
About a man who's reached his end
From the backward progeny of ant.

In the experience of great poets
Some traits proclaim such naturalness
That, having found them, we can't do more
Than end by being completely numb.

Assured of kinship with all things
And with the future closely knit,
We can't but fall—what heresy!—
Into unbelieved simplicity.

But to be spared we can't expect
If we do not conceal it closely.
Men need it more than anything,
But complex things are easier for them . . .

13

October, but the sun's like August,
And the snow, singeing the first hill,
Redoubles the refraction of
The waves that rolling go like waffles.

When it glows like molten platinum
And gleams and glimmers in the foliage,
More black than needles of the larch—
Is that in essence really snow?

It shines like a photo of the moonlight
Which we examine in the afternoon
And imparts the banality of Sochi
To the nature of more modest Kobulet.

Yet it's a sign: the winter's at the door.
Let's pay a tribute to summer's end,
Take leave, and walk upon the shore
And dip our feet in albumen.

14

The pressure of the wind increases,
And figures rise up in the wind.
They rise and, muffled, backwards walk,
And march past waves as on parade.

They review the assembled line of tide,
And vanish then in chimes of foam,
And them, now curving like a horn,
The far horizon greets on meeting.

TO LOVE SOME WOMEN

To love some women is a cross of weight,
But graceful you have no resort to guile:
The secret of your subtle charm equates
The puzzle that perplexes us through life.

Spring in a flurry brings us many dreams
And, rustling, stirs with novelties and truths.
You issue straight from such a pristine stream,
Like April air your meaning's limpid clear.

How easy, waking, to clarify the trouble,
And from the heart shake loose all wordy chaff;
Pursue your life, well-rid of all such rubble.
But living so displays no cunning craft.

THERE'S NO ONE IN THE HOUSE

The house will share no other presence
Save the twilight. The winter day alone
Appears in the transparencies
Where curtains have remained undrawn.

Only the snowflakes whitely blow
And flash in swirling rapid flight.
There's nothing there—just roofs and snow,
The snow and roofs: no man in sight.

The frost again will scratch a line;
And whirling me about again,
Last year's depression will consign
Me to past winters' fuss and pains.

Feelings of guilt again will prick
With never a pardon to their name;
And dearth of firewood, this lack,
Will seize the windows' crosslike frame.

But suddenly along the curtains
Of some intrusion runs the shudder.
And measuring with steps the silence,
You will surprise me like the future.

Surprise me, looming in the doorway,
So very simply garbed in white,
In some material made of such array
As goes to sew those snowflakes bright.

MY VERSES, HURRY

My verses, hurry, hurry quick,
I need you as I never have before.
Turning the corner, there's a house
Where days' succession has been broken,
Where comfort's empty, work has stopped,
And where they weep and think and wait.

Where water's drunk like bitter bromide
Of half-slept nights and restless dreams.
A house where bread's like bitter orach,
A house—but let us hasten there.

Let whirlwind howl in the streets—
But you are rainbow striking crystal,
You're dream and tidings: you I send,
I send you, and that means I love.

O marks round women's necks, implanted
By fetishes that dangled there!
How well I know them, how I clutched them,
Who hung for my dear life upon them.
All my life I have suppressed the cry
Of certainty as to those chains;
But they are mastered by the lie
Of alien beds that have grown cold,
And Bluebeard's image is far more
In strength effective than my labors.

O heritage of Philistines!
The injurious specter of unlove
As fantastic as Gogol's *Viy*,

Comes visiting them in the night,
And by that phantom is disfigured
The natural lot of all best wives.

O what fine courage she displayed
When barely leaving the safe wing
Of her beloved mother—jesting,
Her childish laughter she surrendered
Without a protest or resistance,
Her childlike world and childlike laughter—
The child she was, still free from hurt—
Her worries and preoccupations.

Gogol's *Viy* is a horrifying demon the color of earth with eyelids that hang down to his feet. He appears at the tremendous climax of Gogol's ghost story, *The Viy*.

THE POET

Had I but known what lay in store—
That verse with clotting blood could kill;
Yes, kill, and throttle too, what's more,
And kept untried my debuts still;

I'd said, "O never, never, no!"
To jokes with this dread spore of all;
But long the way I'd still to go,
And shy the heart took up the call.

Now this grey age is Rome—the same,
That stands no quirks, insists no fleet
Applause for actor win acclaim,
But death ungrudging and complete.

So when blind passions lines dictate,
They thrust a slave upon the stage;
Then blood alone beats out his fate—
For art dies choked with swelling rage.

VI.

Early Trains

1943

Spacious Earth

1945

WITH ARTIST'S STUBBORNNESS

(*The Artist 1*)

With artist's stubbornness inborn
My soul agrees, when he is strong:
Men's eyes he shuns—of speech now shorn;
He feels ashamed his books are wrong.

But everyone will know that face.
He missed his chance of hide and seek.
His steps he cannot now retrace.
Though to a cellar he might sneak.

It's no use burying fate in earth.
What then? Uncertain to begin,
But in his lifetime gaining girth,
That's the repute he was to win.

But who is he? His trials late—
In what arena were they staged?
With whom his struggle? What his fate?
A war with his own self he waged.

Like shores made warm when Gulfstream calls,
He's all composed of earthy heat.
Into his lough time carried all
That's since been swept into a heap.

He yearns for freedom, self's repose;
But the years passed dourly away,
And somber clouds above him rose
As he worked hunched against the day.

HE RISES. AGES.

(*The Artist 4*)

He rises. Ages. Gilaty.
Remotely somewhere torches glow.
Who, in his wake, to the tribunal—
Of pointed hoods conducts a row.

Again new ages. Other ages yet.
And ages still to come. Those times,
Into whose ears, still obdurate,
He whispers in his visioned dream:

"My life is no faint-figured draft—
It's something solid teeth will crack on.
And Time indeed will spare my craft
From all the critics' carping combs.

"Is entry barred to this our age?
Be it a citadel or shrine,
My horse I'll spur to face that gate,
And rein it sharply on that line.

"No jesting minstrel or mere bard,
I've made my charger rear up straight,
That I might scan the camp of war,
There, from the highest peaks of fate.

"And barely tugging at the reins,
I'm off haphazard in a rush
Into your passages and lanes,
Which darkness yet surrounds in ambush.

Gilaty—a famous monastery in Georgia, associated with King David
the Builder, and a great cultural and religious center.

"Storm-like, mastering on the way
Both life and passion, chance and death,
Through minds and countries you will stray,
Eternally transmitting faith.

"Your hard campaign will change the place.
Beneath your hooves' strong iron thud,
And scouring clean a tongue-tied race,
New waves of languages will flood.

"The roofs of cities on the way,
And every hovel's humble porch,
Each poplar springing out of clay,
Will learn to recognize your face."

Amazed at heights so sheer,
At Terek's turbid violence,
Inside a flower's blouse
I also crawled—a drone.

Summer 1936

FEARFUL TALE

Soon everything around will change.
The city will be soon rebuilt.
The fright of children rudely wakened
Will impose a lasting guilt.

One cannot forget the fear,
That furrowed all those faces.
The enemy will pay for this
A hundredfold in every case.

His roaring guns will be remembered.
That time will fully be recorded
When he acted arbitrarily,
As Herod did in Bethlehem.

A new and better age will come.
The witnesses will all have gone.
The suffering of small children maimed
By us can never be forgotten.

War Months (*Late 1941*)

OUTCAST

In our garden today there's gloom.
The garden's more lovely each hour.
O even this year—of its bloom
One may drain the draught in this bower.

The man that inhabits this place
No longer feels attached to his home:
His family's gone, and a race
Of invaders at large in the loam.

Alone, now his wife's far from here,
He lingers with neighbors and friends,
As though in their midst he may hear
Some news that a victory sends.

He may stroll in the garden or run
To the local Home Guard depot,
On the way observing the sun
As it sets near Smolensk in a glow.

As evening its beauty relives,
Past Vyazma, Gjatsk, in a hurry,
The highway speeds headlong and heaves
With a five-ton army lorry.

This man's not yet old, nor a figure
Of fun for men younger in strength;
And his shotgun is even younger
By some twenty summers in length.

War Months (*Late 1941*)

THE OLD PARK

A little boy upon a bed.
The raucous roaring of the breeze.
The flights of cawing rooks nine-sped
From peaceful perches on the trees.

A doctor in white gown has called
To scour those wounds, his help extend
The patient quickly grasps it all:
The paternal home, his boyhood friend.

In this old park again he spies
The frosty rime that mornings bring;
And when the bandages are plied,
The panes of weeping windows ring.

The voice of this our present age,
And visions of time past itself,
Are slowly being healed, assuaged,
With careful nurse's soothing help.

Across the ward they come and go
As doors are banged, explosions shake.
The guns roar dully there below
In batteries beyond the lake.

The sun dips low as down it strikes,
Now spitting through a river bank;
And out from there, in lengthy spikes
Of space, it gleamed before it sank.

Then, for a second brief or so,
As from a magic lantern shed,
Waves of emerald overflow
And fill the roadway ruts ahead.

The pangs of pain soon harden to wild groan.
The gusts blow tougher, savage-grown:
The rooks in nines are finally flown,
Like nines of clubs black-fluttering thrown.

The skirling wind now wrenches, sways
The trees, and bends them to the root.
Beneath the branches' moaning lays,
He has forgot his wounded foot.

Traditions helped to age this park:
For here Napoleon had stood,
And "Slav" Samarin left his mark,
And lies here buried in this wood.

The offspring of Decembrists here,
Of Russian heroines grand-nephew,
With petty shots, he scattered rooks
And learnt his Latin to construe.

If strength return, and once more sound,
With his grandpa he will compete:
A Slavophil ancestor found
He will re-edit and complete.

As for himself, he'd write a play
On themes by this great war inspired,
While forests murmured, ceaseless swayed—
So mused he, flat on his sick bed.

War Months (Late 1941)

SUMMER DAY

With us in springtime, until dawn,
In orchards blazing bonfires flame
As pagan altars once had shone
To give fertility acclaim.

The virgin soil is dried and baked,
And steam and vapor from its swarm;
And the whole earth is fire-caked
Like stove-beds kept all winter warm.

When toiling and in earth engrossed,
My shirt I strip and throw away:
With scorching sun my back's then glossed
And baked like some big lump of clay.

And standing pat where heat's most hot,
And with my eyes half in a daze,
From head to foot, upon this spot,
I'm covered with a coat of glaze.

But when the night invades my room,
And I peep from the doorway dimmed—
As jugs are filled, so with the bloom
Of lilac, moisture, I am brimmed.

Night washes off the surface shell
Of walls' cooled evening face,
Presents it to a chosen girl
Who's native born in this small place.

And spreading everywhere in flight,
To freedom it will stretch its powers,
While curling up for rest at night
Upon a painted chest of drawers.

Peredelkino (Early 1941)

THE PINES

On grass, amid the balsams wild,
The forest trees and camomiles,
With arms flung freely back we lie,
Our heads upturned toward the sky.

Amid the pine-tree glade, the grass
Grows thickly woven into fugues:
Our eyes then meet, and we exchange
Our places and our attitudes.

So, for a time become immortal,
We're numbered in the face of pines:
From epidemics, plagues, all ills
And death, we're now for once immune.

In a deliberate moving mass,
Like ointment, the blue-green shadows thick
Make mocking conquest of the grass,
And patch our sleeves with fibres dark.

We share the repose of pine-tree forests:
To restless stir of ants we breathe
The pine glade's sleep-inducing blend
Of laudanum and lemon.

But so fantastic are the spurts
Of trunks sun-fired against blue sky,
That to remove our hands from under
Our upturned heads we'll long delay.

Such spaces spread before our eyes,
And everything seems so submissive,
That somewhere past those tree-trunks, I
Envision constantly the sea.

There, waves rise higher than these branches,
And, tumbling from a rushing roller,
They hurl a hail-hard shower of shrimps,
From the sea's tormented depths upgathered.

But in the evening, taken now in tow,
The setting sun on corks moves further
And shimmers in bright codfish oil
And the dim hue of smoking amber.

The dusk begins to fall, and slowly then
The moon all traces will inter
Beneath the magic white of foam
And blacker magic of the water.

The waves mount higher and more loud,
But the people thronging on the float
A poster on a stand surround,
Undistinguishable from afar.

Peredelkino (Early 1941)

186

FALSE ALARM

The troughs and tubs inane,
The fuss of early hours,
The sunsets and the rains,
The damp of evening showers.

The tears and stifled pains
In sighing dark of day,
The whistling of the trains
Some two-three miles away.

The creeping evening twilight
In garden and in dyke,
The cracks and damage slight—
That's all September-like.

But daytime's autumn furrow
Is rippled with a quiver
When voices, shrill in sorrow,
Lament graves by the river.

And when the widow's sobbing
Comes drifting over the hill,
My heart responds by throbbing,
And then I face death's chill.

Each year when knocks the Fall,
Out of my house I see
The dilatory call
Of my last term's decree.

But having cleared strewn paths,
From that low hillock's eaves
At my life winter stares
Through yellow fright of leaves.

Peredelkino (Early 1941)

HOARFROST

It's the deadest moment of the autumn,
And the geese in wedges have taken wing.
Be not disturbed, there's no good reason:
Fear has the largest eyes of all.

Let the wind that has cradled the rowan
Frighten its nursling ere it close its eyes.
Creation's as subtly deceptive
As a story with a happy ending.

Tomorrow you'll wake from your sleep
And emerging on winter's smooth plain,
Again round the water pump's corner
You will stand as if rooted to earth.

And again those insects so white,
And the roofs, and Father Christmas,
And the chimneys, and the lop-eared forest,
Got up as a clown in masquerade.

In one swoop all is covered with ice
In shaggy fur cap pulled down to the eyes
And, like wolverine creeping in trees,
Watchfully peers from the branches.

You move on ahead with distrust.
The track suddenly dives in ravine.
Here the hoarfrost's a vaulted chamber
With a timber grill gracing the gate.

There, behind the thick curtain of snow,
Stands the wall of some kind of a lodge.
There's a roadway and the fringe of a copse,
And further on a new thicket is seen.

The silence so solemnly reigning,
And anciently patterned in wood,
Resembles the lines of a quatrain
To a princess asleep in a tomb.

To the kingdom so white and so dead
Which sends a sharp shudder through me,
I quietly whisper: "In honor be praised!"
Thou hast given far more than was asked.

Peredelkino (Early 1941)

THE CITY

A wintry kitchen. Petya's piping,
A frozen room and blizzards' waste—
All these may grow past daily bearing,
And leave at last a bitter taste.

The tracks are snowbound past all reason;
And snowdrifts, death and slumber tell
That this is not a proper season,
But of the times the end and knell.

On slippery steps unchipped ice still,
And frosty bands the well chain down.
A magnet draws us in this chill
Toward the warm expectant town.

In winter country life's no life—
I need not stress this or insist:
With unconcern the city's rife
To imperfections that persist.

A thousand fantasies in gyre
He spun, and need not feel the cold;
And, like a ghost, he is inspired
By swarming souls that thronged his fold.

From railway sidings he seems now
To lonely stacks of frozen logs
Just such a vision's distant glow
Amid the night's effulgent fogs.

Although I thought him rather young,
His pertness pleased me anyway.
The tales of history, on his tongue,
Appeared unfinished till his day.

The twinkling stars he loved to ape
With nightly show of promised good,
And even heaven assumed his shape
In boyish dreams that were my mood.

Peredelkino (Early 1941)

ON EARLY TRAINS

Near Moscow living, I, this winter,
In blizzard, chill and snow,
On business when it was essential
Always caught the train to town.

When I went out on some occasions
The street was black as pitch.
And through the forests dark I scattered
My tread that creaked at every step.

Confronting me at the highway crossing
White willows straggled in the waste.
Above, the constellations towered
In January's frozen ditch.

At the backyards, normally
The mail train or Number Forty
Tried hard to overhaul me, but I
Was aiming at the Six O'Clock.

Then the cunning wrinkles of the light
In feelers gathered round.
A searchlight sped full speed upon
The staggered viaduct.

In the compartment's stifling heat,
I gave myself up wholly
To a surge of inborn weakness
I'd sucked in from the breast.

Through all the trials of the past,
The years of war and hardship,
I silently identified
Russia's inimitable features.

Mastering my adoration,
And deifying, I observed:
Here were locksmiths, workers,
Students, and peasant women.

In them I found no servile traits
Such as great need imposes,
And, like any gentlemen, they bore
Discomfort and bad news.

Closely packed as in a carriage,
In every kind of pose,
Adults and children were engrossed
In reading as though wound up.

Then Moscow met us in the gloom
Which sometimes shone like silver,
And leaving the ambiguous light,
We walked out of the subway.

Posterity shoved me to the wall,
And splashed me on the way
With fresh birdcherry soap
And mellifluous honeycake.

Peredelkino (Early 1941)

SPRING AGAIN

The train has gone. The embankment is black.
How shall I find the road in the dark?
The countryside is unrecognizable,
Though I've been absent only twenty-four hours.

The clang of iron has died on the rails.
Suddenly—what is this for a novelty so peculiar?
All the commotion of gossiping chatter. . . .
What devil's got into them?

Where have I heard these fragments of speech
Before on some other occasion last year?
Ah, no doubt, this day once again
A stream has emerged from the thicket at night.
It must be a wier has bulged,
As in former times, and moved the ice along.
Verily, a new miracle this.
As in times gone by, this is spring again.

It is she, it is she.
It is her witchery and wonder.
It is her padded coat behind the willow,
Her shoulders, plait, her gait and back.
It's the snowmaiden on the brink of the precipice.
It is of her that the ravine from its depths
Pours without cease the hurried delirium
Of a half-crazed chatterbox.

Before her, pouring over the barriers,
Those are the rapids drowning in watery fumes,
By the lamp of the suspended waterfall

Hissingly nailed to the steep.
With teeth chattering from the chill,
That's the icy stream cascading over the edge
Into a pond and out of the pond into another vessel.
The floodwaters' speech is the delirium of being.

Peredelkino (Early 1941)

THE THRUSHES

A broody lunch-time silence reigns
   About this station so remote.
Close by the railway, in the lanes,
   Greenfinches sing their lifeless note.

Sultry and boundless as desire
   Is this straight village road and space.
A lilac wood looks all on fire
   Beneath a grey cloud's hair-topped face.

Along a leafy road, the trees
   Engage in play a plodding horse.
In hollows, saying take me please,
   Snow and violets, mould and gorse.

It is from hollows such as these
   That thrushes drink, when in exchange,
With ice and fire in their knees,
   Of rumoured day they ring the change.

Here syllables, now short, now long,
   And here the showers, hot and cold;
Thus throats are fashioned like a gong,
   Brass-lined with puddles sheen and mould.

They have allotments on the stumps,
   Their games of peeping Tom, sly looks,
Their long-day fuss and rowdy romps,
   And chattering in airy nooks.

And dashing through their wide-flung chambers
  Enigmas dart in public rhyme.
Theirs is the clock of drowsy quavers
  And branches chanting quarter-time.

Such is the thrush's shady bower,
  They dwell in woods spared by the rake,
As artists should, tuned to this power.
  Theirs is the way I also take.

Peredelkino (Early 1941)

VII.

A Rift in the Clouds

1955-59

1. IN EVERYTHING I STRIVE

In everything I strive to reach
The very kernel:
In work and in exploring ways,
In pangs of heart.

Down to the essence of spent days,
Their very cause,
Foundations, deepest roots,
The very core.

And grasping at the thread of acts
And destinies,
To live, think, feel and love, and make
Discoveries.

O if I only could explain,
Or even partly,
I'd write a couple of quatrains
On passion's traits.

On lawlessness and sin,
Pursuits, escapes,
The consequence of chance and haste,
And elbows, palms.

Of passion I'd evolve the law
And very principle,
Repeat the first initials of
Its various names.

Like garden soil I'd break up verse.
With all their veins
A-quiver, lindens there would blossom,
In Indian file.

To verse I'd bring the breath of roses,
The breath of mint,
The scent of sedge, mown hay, and meadows,
And peals of thunder.

Thus once upon a time Chopin,
In his *Études*,
Of groves and parks, estates and graves,
The wonder introduced.

The play and trial of elation
Thus achieved,
Is like the bowstring, tightly drawn,
Of a stubborn bow.

2. TO BE THAT FAMOUS IS HARDLY HANDSOME

To be that famous is hardly handsome.
It is not this will raise our score.
No need to pay the archives' ransom
Or loss of manuscripts deplore.

Creation's aim—yourself to give,
Not loud success, appreciation.
To mean round nothing—shames to live,
On all men's lips an empty sermon.

But we should live without pretending,
So live that, in the final count,
We win the love of space unending,
And future's voice our utterance haunt.

If gaps must be, let gaps be rife
In destiny and not on paper,
In margins only marking life's
Completed passages and chapters.

Of the unknown we should embrace
The wager, there one's steps conceal
As mist might wrap away some place
When not a jot is to be seen.

While men will track your vital trail,
Retracing step by step your feet,
You must inevitably fail
To tell your triumph from defeat.

Nor must you even by a hair
Retreat to spite your living face,
But prove as quick and, this your share,
Stay quick, the quickest in your race.

1956

3. THE SOUL

My soul, my little mourner,
That grievst for all good friends,
Thou hast become endrowser
Of those who live in pain.

Their bodies stiff embalming,
To them devoting verse,
With trembling lyre sobbing,
Thou weepest their demise.

In our mean-centered time,
As conscience, guardian best,
Thou standst a funeral urn
Wherein their ashes rest.

Their sufferings all told
To earth have bowed thee down.
Thou reekest of charnel mold,
Of mortuaries and tombs.

My soul, my charnel house,
All things we've witnessed here,
Mill-ground without a truce,
Thou turnest into pulp.

Go on, and further grind
My whole life's way and toil,
Some forty years in kind,
Into a graveyard soil.

4. EVE

By water's edge tall trees now stand.
And from a hill nearby the summer day
Has tossed the clouds into the pond,
Like men their ample dragnets ply.

The sky's as heavy as a sweep-net;
Now plunging in, a crowd of bathers
Invades these skies as though a net:
Men, women, children, all together.

Then, from a thicket, five-six women
Move to the beach and without fuss
Wring out upon the scorching sand
The dripping water from their suits.

And like an adder writhing forward,
The curling yarns now twist, now crawl,
As if the serpent and the tempter
Had hid inside the knitted cloth.

O woman, your appearance, glance,
In no wise baffle me or trip.
You're like a throat that bulges tense
When seized by feeling in its grip.

You were created in rough draft,
A line from another cycle taken,
Or as in sleep, all jokes apart,
You from my rib had now uprisen.

At once eluding hands that grasp,
You slipped away from my embrace—
The very shudder and the gasp,
And of man's heart the sudden spasm.

5. WITHOUT A TITLE

So unapproachable, subdued,
Today you're fire and burning flame.
O let me lock away your beauty
In the darkling chamber of a poem.

Behold how all things grow transformed
By lampshade's lucent skin of fire:
The wall and windows' edge, this room,
Our shadows and our figures here.

You sit with legs crossed like a Turk
Upon an ottoman at ease.
It's all the same—in light or dark,
You always reason like a child.

Conversing, a heap of beads you thread
Which had scattered from your neck.
What sadness in your glance I read;
Your words are too direct, naive.

"Love" has become a trivial word,
You're right; another name for you
I'll find. The whole wide world, all words,
For your dear sake, I'll name anew.

How can your frowning looks convey
Of your emotions the rich core,
Your heart's bright glowing secret layer?!
What makes your eyes so sadly stare?

1956

6. CHANGE

To paupers I was once inclined
From no ideal consideration,
But simply that I there did find
Life less parade or ostentation.

Although I knew the lordly ways
And manner of folk who were refined,
I was the foe of parasites
And friend of vagrants much maligned.

I always tried to make good friends
With men who labored for their bread,
For which I was in honor paid
By being dubbed a ragamuffin.

The look of cellars unembellished,
Of attics with no curtains hung,
Was firm without descriptive relish,
Quite sturdy, tangible, imposing.

But since those days I too am spoilt
When time had fallen to corruption,
And grief was elevated "shame,"
To mime the optimists' intention.

To all whom I had always trusted,
I have long since become untrue.
Man is the loss I have sustained
Since everybody's lost him too.

1956

7. SPRING IN THE FOREST

The weather, desperately cold,
Obstructs the seasonable thaw.
The spring lags longer than of old,
And proves more careless even so.

The rooster preens himself in lust:
The hen will try in vain to run.
A pine tree, turning to face south,
Screws up its eyes at the forceful sun.

Although the ground now steams and stews,
For many days and weeks ahead
The roads are fettered by the ice
And with black bark are overlaid.

The forest's heaped with trash of fir,
And snow abundantly tops all.
And where the thaw has tried to stir,
There's sun and water nearly equal.

The sky in clouds as in down
Above black vernal puddles shined
Fast stuck where branches high abound,
By sudden heat immobilized.

8. SUMMER

About the house a ghost is stalking.
All day his steps sound overhead.
Across the attic shadows flitting,
And in the house a specter's tread.

He walks in everywhere intruding,
And pokes his nose in all affairs;
Toward the bed he steals in dressing-
Gown, and the table-cloth from table tears.

He fails to wipe his feet when entering,
And rushing in with whirling gust,
He with the curtain, to the ceiling,
As with a dancer leaps aloft.

But who is this so rude and spoilt,
This double of you, specter, ghost?
This ghost's our lodger, new arrival,
This phantom is our summer guest.

For his brief holiday entire
We have sublet to him our house.
July, the stormer, July's air,
Has rented all our rooms from us.

July, who carries in his clothes
The dandelions' down, and thistles' too;
July, a traveler through windows,
Who speaks in thunder openly.

A tousled lad unkempt from the steppe,
Of lindens smelling and the grass,
In beet and dill and scallions steeped,
Air of July, air of the fields.

1956

9. AUTUMN DAY

We're gone to gather mushrooms.
A highway. Forests. Ditches.
Along the road, to left
And right, the telegraph poles.

From highway wide we plunge
Into a forest dark.
Then ankle-deep in dew,
We wander all spread out.

The sun from forest fringe,
Through labyrinthine darkness,
Throws filtered light on toadstools,
On mushrooms brown under bushes.

A stump that masks a mushroom.
A bird alights on it.
A shadow serves as landmark
That we might keep our way.

But, in September, time
Is measured out so strict,
That hardly will the dawn
Break through to reach us here.

The hampers are well-stuffed.
The baskets very full.
All pine-mushrooms here,
A half of them at least.

We go. Behind our back
The forest wall's unmoving
Where day in earthly beauty
Was prematurely burnt.

1956

10. SILENCE

Suffused with sun, the forest glows.
The sunbeams rise in pillared dust.
From here, they say, an elk steps slow
And walks upon the roads that cross.

The forest's absolutely hushed,
As though the life of that deep dell
Were by the gleaming sun not ambushed,
But mastered by another spell.

It's really so: there, not too far,
The elk stands rooted in the brush.
The trees, at her, dumbfounded stare.
That's why the forest is so hushed.

The elk starts nibbling at young shoots,
With crunching teeth nips them all level.
Caught on its crest, from roots upraised,
On a branch above an acorn dangles.

Ox-daisy, St.-John's-wort, rosebay,
And thistle, cow-wheat, camomile,
Entangled in some spell of fey,
Look glazed around the bushes' aisle.

In this wide forest, in a gully,
One stream alone, mellifluously bent
Repeats now quietly, now loudly,
The tale of this so fabulous event.

Thus dinning in this forest dell,
Addressing a stray woodman there,
Some tiding to him it would tell
In words quite human to the ear.

1956

11. HAYRICKS

The purple dragon-flies now scurry,
And bumble-bees buzz here and there.
The *Kolhoz* maidens laugh from wagons,
And choppers pass with scythes on shoulder.

The while good weather holds the day,
They busily rake and turn the fodder
And pile it up before sun sets
In hayricks quite as large as houses.

Before the sun goes down, a hayrick
Begins to looks like a coaching inn.
Where night has slumped upon its berth
Of heaped-up hay and clover mown.

When shadows fade toward the morning,
A hayrick towers like a hayloft,
In which the moon, when passing by,
Had dived and spent the night asleep.

No sooner light than wagon follows wagon
Through meadows, rolling in the dark.
The dawning day gets up from rest
With trash and hay mixed in its hair.

At noon the heights again gleam blue.
Again the hayricks rear like clouds;
The earth again, like anisette,
Gives evidence of strength and fragrance.

12. THE LINDEN ALLEY

A gateway with a rounded arch.
Then hillocks, meadows, forests, oats.
In evening air, inside the park,
A house of beauty unforeseen.

There linden trees of goodly girth
In dusk of alleys celebrate,
Their crests concealed behind each other,
Their bicentennial jubilee.

High they join their vaults together.
Below—a sward and flower garden,
Which paths, correctly instituted,
Cut at right angles straight ahead.

Beneath the lindens, as underground,
No speck of light shines in the sand,
But there's a glimmer in the distance
As though it beamed from tunnel's mouth.

But then the days of budding come,
And lindens, by their foliage girt,
Now scatter, also with their shade,
An irresistible aroma.

The strollers in their summer hats
Breathe in—whoever near may stand—
This unfathomable scent
Which bees alone can understand.

He composes in these instants,
When he grips you by the heart,
A volume's content and its theme—
The park and flowerbeds its binding.

Upon an ancient, cumbrous tree,
Which curtains off the house above,
There burns, with dripping wax besmeared,
The flowers which the fire had lit.

1956

13. A RIFT IN THE CLOUDS

A plate the lake so large resembles.
Beyond it clouds now congregate
In towering heaps of white assembled
Where frowning glaciers concentrate.

As light keeps changing all the while,
The forest alters in its hue.
Now all ablaze, now with black piles
Of clinging soot it's covered too.

When, at the close of rainy days,
The azure through the clouds will seep,
How festive momently the sky!
How full of awe the grass replete!

The wind drops down, horizons purging.
The sun on earth spills all its mass.
The leaves in gleaming green are shining
Like images upon stained glass.

From windows, drawn on varied glass,
Into eternity they stare:
The hermit, emperor and saint—and pass,
Their sleepless halos twinkling there.

Within, this vast cathedral dim
Appears to covet earth's extent;
Remote, I sometimes catch the drone
Of choir ascending to a chant.

O world, O universe, O nature,
Mysterious source—prolonged your service
I'll endure, shot with a holy tremor
And bathed in tears of happiness.

1956

14. BREAD

For decades you've collected conclusions,
But you've never inscribed them on paper;
And if you're not maimed by confusion,
You ought to have grasped at least something.

You have grasped the bliss of pursuits,
Of success the secret and law;
You've grasped that to loaf is a curse,
That joy is not won without deeds.

That the somber princedom of plants,
Of mysterious lairs and wild beasts,
Awaits its heroes and champions,
Its altars and revelations.

That of all such revelations,
There remains, in destiny's chain,
The bread that was nurtured through ages
As a forefather's gift to his sons.

That a field of ripe wheat or of rye
Not only demands to be threshed,
But that once in the past this same page
Your ancestor recorded of you.

That this is indeed his true word,
His unrecedented beginning
In the midst of all life on the earth,
Of all births and labors and deaths.

15. THE AUTUMN FOREST

The autumn forest's like a blanket.
So stuffed with silence, shade and sleep.
No squirrel, owl or woodpecker
Will wake it from its slumber deep.

Along those autumn paths, the sun,
When it adventures in at close of day,
Will move in fearfulness alert
Lest it may fall into a snare.

Inside are swamps and stumps and aspens,
And alder thickets, spreading moss;
And somewhere past the forest fens,
The village cocks are crowing hoarse.

A cock will raise a raucous shout;
Then silence dominates again
As if, immersed in deepest thought,
He puzzles the meaning of his strain.

But somewhere else and more remote
A neighboring cock bawls out reply;
And like a watchman on his beat,
Our cock will answer to his cry.

Like certain echo, he'll respond;
And all the cocks with little rest
Will hoarsely mark, as with a bond,
Both North and South, and East and West.

Upon this clamoring exchange,
The forest opens wide its ranks
And spies the unaccustomed range
Of fields, horizons and blue skies.

16. FIRST FROSTS

One chilly morning when the sun was dim
And stood a fiery pillar in the smoke,
I too was hardly visible to him
When seen as in a photograph all blurred.

Until the sun comes striding out of gloom,
And lights the meadow past the pond,
The view trees have of me is very dim
As on the pond's most distant edge I stand.

Man's recognition always comes much later—
Once he has passed and plunged into the mist.
A layer of gooseflesh covered biting frost;
The air looked falser than a film of rouge.

You walked upon the hoarfrost of a path
As on a muffling stretch of mat.
To bear this chill the earth is very loathe,
Nor can it breathe potatoes in a patch.

17. NIGHT WIND

The songs and drunken shouts subside.
Tomorrow early we shall rise.
In huts the lights go out. The tribe
Of youth have scattered to their homes.

The wind alone still reels about,
Threading again the same wild track
Where with a crowd of merry lads
He by himself did journey back.

His head droops low behind the door.
Disliking these nocturnal riots,
He'd rather patch a good accord,
Night's disagreements turn to quiet.

In front, a garden palisade.
Disputing, they still sign no peace.
The trees upon the road debate
In throng their points of difference.

1957

18. FOUL WEATHER

The rain has mired all the roads;
The wind keeps cutting them like glass.
The wind from willows strips their load
And clips them all extremely close.

Some mourners from a graveyard ride
While fluttering leaves to earth fall flop.
A sweaty tractor with an eight-
Toothed harrow ploughs the winter crop.

The leaves, in a black and winding furrow,
Into a pond come whirling down,
And in a stir of ripples follow
Like ships maneuvering in line.

The rain beats spattering on a sieve.
The cold would clamp us in a brace.
With shame all things are covered over—
As though this autumn brought disgrace.

It seems, abuse and shame and pain
Fly mingled with the leaves and ravens,
With driving rain and hurricane
That on all sides on us thrash down.

19. WIND

(*Some Fragments About Blok*)

I

Who will survive and be accepted,
Who censured and accounted dead,
Such is the province of our toadies—
Of them alone, empowered thus.

No one would know, let us assume,
That Pushkin's honored or indited
Without their doctoral dissertations
Which throw on all things so much light.

But Blok, thank God, is different;
His essay is of different kind:
From Sinai he did not descend,
Adopting us his rightful heirs.

For fame depending on no lecture,
No schools or systems deemed eternal,
He has escaped all manufacture,
And no one thrusts him down our throat.

Alexander Blok (1880-1921), greatest Russian Symbolist poet. His masterpiece is *The Twelve*, an epic of the Soviet Revolution (1918).

20.

2

He is windy as wind. And like the wind
That whistled on the estate in days
When Filka the polisher of floors
Still galloped with his buffing wheel.

The Jacobin grandfather was still alive,
A radical of crystalline soul,
And his windy grandson did not lag
Behind him by a finger's length.

That wind, which seeped beneath the ribs
And into the soul as years went by,
Is mentioned both in ill and good repute
In verses where it's celebrated.

That wind is everywhere. In the house,
In trees, in the village, in the rain,
In the poetry of his third volume,
In *The Twelve*, in death, everywhere . . .

21.

3

The horizon is curt and malevolent,
And all bruised and bloody the dawn,
Like the marks of raw scratches unhealed
Or a reaper with blood on his feet.

There is no counting the clefts in the sky,
Those forerunners of tempests and ills,
And with reeking stagnation, iron and rust,
The air of the swamps is all filled.

When in forest, on road, in ravine,
In a village of size or a hamlet,
In the clouds such zig-zags are seen,
They portend bad weather and trials on earth.

When over a capital city
The sky glimmers purple and rust,
Then the State's on the brink of disaster,
And a hurricane threatens the land.

These schisms Blok could read in the sky.
The firmament served to foretell
Violent tempests and terrible weather
A grandiose storm and a cyclone.

Blok expected this storm and upheaval.
Its brush strokes of violence and fire,
With their fear and their thirst of the issue,
Made their mark on his life and his verse.

22. AFTER A BREAK

Three months ago, when early blizzards
Unleashed their newly gathered fury
And against our unprotected garden
With savage desperation hurried;

I misled myself when I pretended
That, like a convict, I would hide
And writing of winter as intended,
My springtime volume would complete.

But trifles manifold upon
Me tumbled like snowdrifts in a mound.
The winter, contrary to plan,
Was almost half gone round.

At last I really understood
Why—when the snow had always fallen
And snowflakes pierced the somber shroud—
It always spied in from the garden.

With lips white-frosted from the chill,
It whispered urgently: "Make haste!"
But sharpening pencils all the while,
I still repeated my excuse.

As I malingered under the lamp
One morning early at my task,
That winter came and then decamped—
A reminder I had failed to grasp.

23. FIRST SNOW

Outside, the blizzard rages,
On all things casting gloss.
The news-vendor's powdered white,
And from sight the kiosk's lost.

In the course of our long existence
It often seemed to us
That the snow falls out of secrecy
And to mislead the eyes.

O snow, impenitent concealer—
Beneath a fringe of white,
How often from outlying suburbs
Did he conduct us home!

When all is bundled in white flakes,
And snow quite glues the eyes,
Then, groping like a drunkard,
A shadow stalks the yard.

Its movements here are rather hurried.
And then again it's certain
That someone feels he must conceal
Some very sinful thing.

The snow will fall—a shudder will shake
The window, palisade,
But the knots his fingers ravelled
Can never be unmade.

1956

24. SNOW FALLS

Snow is falling, falling snow.
Toward white stars in whirling storm
Geraniums stretch nostalgically,
Behind a window's barricade.

The snow is falling, all's confusion,
All things far-whirling take to flight.
The staircase steps so black, so black,
And sidestreets branching left and right.

The snow is falling, falling snow.
Looks as if no flakes were falling,
But in a patched and cumbrous coat
The sky in person to earth descending.

Resembling someone's looks eccentric
From the highest landing of the stair,
Creeping, playing hide and seek,
The sky descends from attic lair.

Since life will never stay and wait,
Before you've time to turn—it's Yule.
A brief pause in between, and straight
We're celebrating the New Year.

Thickly falling, falling snow,
Keep step with it, and with those feet,
In that same tempo moving slow
Or hurry almost quite as fast.

Time itself will pass by here perhaps?
As snow comes falling, is it true
The next year runs the same tried laps?
Or as in a poem words pursue?

Snow is falling, falling snow.
Snow is falling, all's confused—
A passerby shows snow-white now,
In windows plans are much surprised,
Roads meet and sidestreets turning go.

25. FOOTPRINTS IN THE SNOW

Slantingly across the fields
A girl's prints move through snow to sunset.
From one wide common to another
Her boots of felt leave their smudged trace.

A child clings closer to its nurse.
A sunbeam like some lemonade
Has trickled into holes and hollows
And lies in ice the hue of puddles.

It chills there in the dripping ooze
Of an egg inside a broken shell,
And a pair of skis with their blue line
Divide it on the path in half.

The moon, like pancake, slides in cream,
Slithering sideways all the time.
A sleigh comes speeding in pursuit,
But there's no catching the slipping ball.

26. AFTER THE BLIZZARD

After the blizzard's rage has settled down,
The surrounding country breathes in calm.
And at my leisure, then, I love to listen
To children shouting by the frozen stream.

Most likely I am wrong and quite mistaken;
I must be blind or really rather mad.
The winter, like a plaster cast of woman,
All dead and white, falls earthward in the wind.

From overhead the sky admires the molding
Of those blank eyes so deeply pressed and lifeless.
The yard, each stick—snow covers everything—
Each little shoot upon the trees.

The river's ice, the crossing, the platform pale,
The forest, rails, embankment, and the booth,
All these are cast in forms immaculate,
With edges rough and corners rounded smooth.

At night, before forgetting all in sleep,
In lucid moment from my sofa rising,
Upon a page I place a world's wide sweep
And hold it there in a quatrain confining.

The stumps and snags resemble sculptured figures
As bushes do that line the river now.
I try to build a sea of roofs on paper—
A world entire, a city in the snow.

27. BACCHANALIA

The city. A winter sky.
Darkness. The portals yawn.
At Boris-and-at-Gleb's
Shines light: the mass is on.

Brows in prayer knit,
Halos, old women's shushes . . .
All this quite dimly lit
By candleflame held low.

The blizzard in the street
Blankets all things together,
Allows no man to meet—
Hard though they try to get together.

A wild and swirling storm
Blots everything in sight:
The jail, the excavators,
Cranes, building on old sites.

Wisps of repertoire
Flap in the wind like rags—
And trees upon the boulevard
Like silver filigree.

The signs of a great age—
At every step we know
In turmoil and rampage
And tire-marks on the snow.

In shifty looks—the signs
Of landmarks changing fast,
The way our friends opine,
Antennas, clouds of masts.

In costumes and facades,
In plainness unadorned
In talk, opinions, fads,
Which affect the heart.

28. BEHIND THE TURNING

Alert, its watchful vigil keeping
At thicket's entrance
A little bird entices, twittering
Lightly on a branch.

It continues chirruping and singing
On a forest's threshold,
As though to forest burrows guarding
The approaches.

Beneath it lie the branches broken;
Above—the clouds.
Around the corner, in a ravine,
The springs and steeps.

Conglomerated logs and stumps
Here crowd the ground.
In oozy meres and chilly swamps
The snowdrops bloom.

But this small bird believes its warble,
As though an oath,
Allows no person undesirable
Across the threshold.

Around the turning, in the depths
Of forest gully,
The future waits prepared, more certain
Than guarantee.

One can't provoke it to dispute
Nor sweeten it.
It stretches deep and spreads out wide,
Like pine-tree woods.

29. EVERYTHING HAS COME TO PASS

The roads have turned to porridge.
I move on, keeping to the side.
The clay and ice, like dough, I squash,
And wade through squelching mire.

Then stridently a jay whirs by
Into a vacant wood of birch.
Like a construction incomplete,
It rises up untenanted.

Now through its clearings I can see
The whole of future life transparent.
All things to the very least degree
Have there been justified, made be.

The wood I enter; I'm in no haste.
In layers the snow-crust now subsides.
As to a bird, the echo answers,
And a whole wide world yields me the way.

Amid this soil of sand and clay,
Which shows the bottom ground beneath,
A small bird chirrups on the sly
Pausing some seconds in between.

As to a music box that's wound,
The forest listens concentrated,
Then resonantly lifts its voice
And waits a time for sound to fade.

30. PLOUGHLANDS

What happened to this landscape so familiar?
Between the earth and sky the frontier's razed.
Ploughed fields, spread out like chessboard squares,
Unfold to the horizon on all sides.

The spacious stretch of ground, freshly harrowed,
Has settled down so smoothly in the distance
One might think the mountains had been levelled
Or all the plains swept tidily for instance.

In these days too, by single spirit moved,
The trees that skirt the furrowed fields
Have blossomed green and early with fresh down
And stand to their full height erectly drawn.

On maples fresh no speck of dust is seen,
And there's no color clearer in the world
Than birch trees' hue of lightest green
Or yonder ploughlands' play of light-gray color.

May, 1958

31. JOURNEY

At full steam the train is rushing.
The wheels of locomotive spin,
The surrounding forest's resinous
And there's something more ahead,
And birch trees cover all the incline.

The track runs on with poles outspread,
Dishevels the woman conductor's curls,
And the air grows far more acid
From fumes that fall upon the slope.

The cylinder and pistons frenzied churn,
And the connecting rod keeps flashing,
And a hawk skims by like a shadow
Alongside the track of railway stretching.

The engine utters sighs in smoke
That sits, a rakish cap, upon it.
But as in days of old King Cole,
And various other ages past,
The forest, heedless of this fuss,
Stands dreaming in our present decade.

And somewhere, somewhere, many cities
Loom remote, as always was the case,
Where in the evening wearily
At some old station trains pull up,
Unloading a throng of new arrivals.

Thither passengers now crowd,
Disgorging from the station yard
Watchmen, travelers, cashiers,
Conductors, engine drivers too.

And then with secrecy especial
The train moves past the curving street
Which elevates the stony cubes
Of boulders stacked upon another.
Then posters, niches, chimneys, roofs,
Clubs, hotels, theaters, shops,
Squares and boulevards, linden trees,
Courtyards, gateways, lodgings, rooms,
Apartments, porches, and staircases,
Where all the passions now compete
How best to alter this old world.

July, 1958

32. WOMEN IN MY CHILDHOOD

In childhood, as I now remember,
From an open window you might lean,
Discovering that the street, like quarry,
Was dark at midday under the trees.

The double poplars, in their shade,
Embraced the whole length of the street:
The sidewalk, pavement and the basements,
The church, with cupolas, to left.

Behind the gate, some paths quite sullen
Conducted one into a garden:
The female element, when present,
Gave life an enigmatic spice.

The girls next door were quite besieged
With girl-friends and acquaintances,
And bird-cherry in clustered bloom
Washed with their leaves the frames of transoms.

Of adult women who, in rage
Abusing others in language plain,
Rose up in doorways like the trees
That border flowering city gardens.

One felt obliged, like a beech tree frowning,
To bear with women's twitter-scourge!—
Thus learn I might profess the passion
And adoration too—heroic urge.

July, 1958

33. THE AIR'S SONOROUS WITH THE STORM DEPARTED

The air's sonorous with the storm departed.
Here, as in Eden, all's alive and breathing blithe.
With broken mauve of branches thickly clustered
To drink the freshened air the lilac strives.

All is made quick by weather's alteration.
With rain the gutters of tin roofs are brimmed,
But ever brighter show the sky's transitions
And zenith blue above the cloud's black rim.

The artist's hand, more masterful in power,
From all things purges dust and dirt.
From his own vats of dye, transfigured more,
Reality and life rise fable-girt.

The fifty years that have in tempest passed,
Fade in the memory fainter every day.
And as our century matures at last,
We to the future must give right of way.

So neither cataclysms nor upheavals
Can cleanse a path to usher life's new claim,
But what is shown in generous traits and trials
Of some man's soul aspiring to flame.

34. WINTER HOLIDAYS

It's not enough to own the future:
The old can hardly satisfy.
We need eternity moreover
To rise tree-bright on Christmas Eve.

That a hostess may bestrew with stars
Her dress and make it glow resplendent.
That sister, brother, from afar
Might flock together for the feast.

Whatever chains you try to hook,
Or pains on *maquillage* expend,
The tree surprisingly still looks
Half-dressed or naked to the end.

More daubed than any chimney sweep,
With hair all ruffled in wisps of smoke,
The festive tree's puffed out, sweet lady,
In several skirts bouffant in shape.

The faces turning more to stone,
A shudder ripples over the candles.
The rivulets of kindled flame
Compress the lips into a heart.

.   .   .   .

The company sits up till dawn.
Then shaking rudely from the snores,
The house, like a shack that's tumbling down,
Keeps slamming a cupboard's little door.

New twilight catches up at last,
And day in stature does diminish.
The guests, still sleeping, miss their breakfast,
But wake in time to dine with relish.

The sun, now settling, like a drunkard
From afar, with quite transparent aim,
Through window stretching out its hand,
For bread and brandy stakes its claim.

Falling, the monster thrust its dial,
All swollen and bloated, in the snow—
The color of a cranberry cordial—
And slumped in embers' dying glow.

January 1959

35. THE NOBEL PRIZE

I am lost like a beast tracked down.
Somewhere men live in freedom and light,
But the furious chase closes in,
And I cannot break out from my plight.

A dark forest, the edge of a pond,
And a log of fir-tree uprooted.
To the world my escape has been cut.
Then befall, what to me is allotted.

What so dreadful a deed have I dared?
Am I a murderer then or a bandit?
To oblige the wide world to shed tears
At the beauty of my native land.

So be it! On the brink of the grave,
I believe in a time very near
When the spirit of good that men crave
Will prove stronger than evil and fear.

January 1959

36. THE WIDE WIDE WORLD

The shades of evening finer than a hair
Grope their way longingly behind the trees.
On the forest path I meet a woman carrier
From the post who handed me a wrapper: "Please!"

Along those tracks that fox and cat prefer,
Along those tracks that cat and fox frequent,
I'm bound for home with this new batch of letters,
And, once arrived, to joy I there give vent.

Foreign countries, mountains, lakes and frontiers
Far-off isthmuses, great continents,
Reports, debates, discussions and reviews,
Young children, older men, and adolescents.

Letters from men, epistles reverend!
Each of your number shows the evidence
Of daily reasoned thought without exception,
And testifies to marked intelligence.

Epistles from the women, precious letters!
I too have tumbled from the clouds.
Henceforth, I swear my loyalty is firmer
In serving you in all men's sight forever.

And as for you, you race of stamp collectors!
For one so brief and cordial rendezvous
O for what gift indeed you'd be the wiser
If in my place you wore my wretched shoes.

January 1959

37. THE ONLY DAYS

For the duration of many winters
I recall the solstice and its days;
Each day was quite unlike another,
Recurred anew in every way.

And of their consequence the train
Produced a pattern drop by drop—
Of days unique in this long chain
When time for us appeared to stop.

I can tell them thoroughly:
The winter halfway through its race;
The roads were sodden, rain dripped slyly,
The sun was bathing on the ice.

As in a dream, the lovers haste
To lock themselves in an embrace,
And on the trees' high-crowning crest
The coops of starlings sweat from heat.

The drowsy hands of clock delay
To make their round on the dial;
And longer than an age this day,
And that embrace which does not fail.

ON MODESTY AND BOLDNESS

Speech of Boris Pasternak at the Writers' Plenum in Minsk, February, 1936

Comrades, I also am excited like the speakers who preceded me. If I may say so, Asseyev was nearest to my excitement when he spoke of Bielorussia, of Bielorussian poetry; when he spoke of that joy which is evoked by the close relationship of the two languages.

When on my way here, I was overjoyed chiefly by the prospect of meeting Iacub Kolas, Ianko Kupala, and Alexandrovich. I shall confine myself for the present by offering my sincere thanks for their existence [*Applause*] and for their being so pure and real.

When thinking of them, the names of Koltzov and Nikitin came into my mind. In this connection, I had intended to speak of folk poetry. But I have followed the debates of the last few days so closely and with such attention that, having gradually absorbed them, I have lost my original urge. Instead, there has accumulated in me other subject matter which it would be useful to discuss dryly on a somewhat lower plane.

When Italy attacked Abyssinia, *Izvestia* printed an excerpt from Tolstoy's diary of 1906, which was written, I think, at the time of Italy's first attack on Abyssinia. I read those excerpts and was shaken by the resemblance of Tolstoy's language concerning these problems to that of Lenin. I recall this because I value this resemblance which, though it may be illusory and fanciful in substance, is yet striking in its tone and in the bluntness with which Tolstoy attacks the venerated and accepted conventions of the Philistine civilization of imperialism.

In her speech about Mayakovsky, Mustangova postulated a broad statement about the authentic predecessors of our present-day poetry; and she did so from a carefully pondered theoretical basis and in a more indisputable way. Following her at an unexpected tangent, I should like to remind you that our Socialist Realism could not have fallen from heaven ready-made, that here too we might find roots over and above those which have been sufficiently studied and which are known to all. Therefore it seems to me personally that the part of annunciation here is shared equally in this respect by both Tolstoy and Maxim Gorky; or, to be more exact, by the stormy nature of Tolstoy's exposures and unceremonious ways. Personally, I think that somewhere here lies that saving tradition, in the light of which everything noisily high-pitched and rhetorical appears unfounded, useless, and, at times, even morally suspicious.

In the last few years, it seems to me that we writers, in our banqueting manner, have strongly departed from this tradition and, in our eloquent advocacy, have been, as it were, waiting for some new Tolstoy nurtured this time by the Socialist revolution—here Alexey Tolstoy immediately suggests himself—who would present us, socialist realists, at the Plenum in the framework of some new "Fruits of Enlightenment."

It is from this very point of view that I very much like Surkov's report. It had in it far less of that high-pitched, bugling triviality, to which we have become so much accustomed that everyone seems to think it obligatory.

Let us speak the truth, comrades: we ourselves are much to blame in many things. For not everything in the world is constructed deductively from somewhere on high. Each stratum of society has its own life and is partially to blame for the nature of its own deposits. We are continuously burdening ourselves with additional fetters which no one wants and which no one demands. We are asked to speed up, but we keep swearing oaths of loyalty instead. Svetlov spoke very well about this.

With rare exceptions, very few of the speakers talked calmly, soberly, to the point. True, it is impossible to fulfill that task, namely, to discuss in the framework of the Plenum the very foundations of art, even if each one of us were given an hour to speak. There are many out-of-date prejudices and preconceived opinions. The analysis of these delusions—errors—would take a whole lifetime, which would be difficult enough, but that has become even more complicated from another angle. Many erroneous views have become dogmas because they are always affirmed jointly with some other point infallible or even sacred; and, in such cases, the effect of this is to make it look as if a part of the *bliss* of these absolute infallibilities had been transferred to those assertions which are far from obligatory to everyone.

Bezimensky, for example, began his speech by referring to such things as the revolution, the mass, soviet society; and, then, not without demagogy, he passed on to rebukes, accusing me, as it were, of something "anti-soviet"—of the fact that I "do not travel and read my poetry" (his expression). But what if I do not do this precisely because I respect the age in which we are living and which has matured to the need of more authentic and more serious forms? What if I consider that my merit lies precisely in what seems incomprehensible to Bezimensky? And what if I had once been enthralled, for example, by the way Pushkin and Tyutchev used to travel and still travel through their books; and what if I had devoted all the energy of my heart to the difficulties of *these* travels at the expense of the easy platform visits, which with us have taken excessive root.

Comrades, a long, long time ago, in about the year 1922, I was already ashamed by the easily available platform victories. It was enough to mount the tribune then to evoke applause. I felt that I was facing the possibility of the birth of a sort of secondary life, revolting in its cheap, false and artificial glitter; and this realization pushed me away from this path. I saw that my role lay in helping the rebirth of the poetic book with pages that spoke with all the force of their deafening muteness; and I began to model myself on higher examples.

Comrades, if we tolerate the orgies of platform readings which, in their circus development, reach at times an absolutely savage level, it is only because in this connection, that is, as a platform phenomenon, Mayakovsky was so vitally true and gave us so astoundingly much that he justified, as it were, for several generations ahead this field of endeavor, having expiated in advance the sins of many future music-hall heroes.

I was very astonished to hear my name so often repeated at this Plenum. Comrades, I am not to blame for that. I do not understand these tendencies. Personally, I have given no cause for these exaggerations. Like each one of you, I represent something real. I am not transparent. I am a body in space. But among us are many jolly fellows with an extremely developed platform imagination. In their imagination, not I alone, but any object, grows into a mountain of trivialities. You yourselves have witnessed such statements. Am I responsible for Bezimensky, who sees life, art, man's destiny, and his own part in all this in precisely this and no other way?

Am I responsible for the elegance with which Vera

Inber has divided the history of mankind into two principal parts after accounting for the resolution of all the alarms and sorrows which, in her opinion, are unthinkable in our midst, upon the geometrical sketch on the frosted window of a tramcar?

Utkin himself, who is far from being my idol and who is in no sense a well-wisher of mine, commented, when protesting against the analysis of his verse undertaken by Vera Inber, that it would seem she did not like the way he had killed off one of his characters in his verse and that she would do it in another way. In defense of Vera Inber, it must be said that she is not alone in this. With few exceptions, everyone here was analyzing lines and stanzas as if they were real events or blunders committed through carelessness or, at best, as vivid or non-vivid anecdotes. But, comrades, the *feuilleton* is merely a genre and, however current it may be in our day, it is far from being an obligatory philosophical system for us.

In general, verse writing was here discussed like the work of some continuously functioning apparatus with a production proportionally related to the labor applied to it. I saw the image of a water pump which, despite every effort, was still lagging behind the general need. But everyone here took an oath: we'll make the effort and, clearly, more water will flow, and we can rest assured about our poetic future.

But seriously now, comrades, I just fail in many respects to understand some of the speakers—we speak a different language. Here, for example, some of you with great conviction distinguished good verses from bad as if they were correctly or incorrectly turned machine parts. Meanwhile, under the guise of bad verse, examples were given of verse that was not even bad, but simply in bad taste, and not accidentally so from the moral standpoint; and I became convinced once again that, generally speaking, verses, good and bad, do not exist, but that there are only good and bad poets, that is, whole systems of thought which are either productive or which spin in the void. And the Stakhanovite promises on the part of the latter are capable of only depressing us.

The German poet, Johannes Becher, and Semeon Kirsanov spoke best of all and with sincere and fruitful emotion about the Stakhanovites. To what they said I should like to add one thing: that surprise is the greatest gift which life can grant us. There should be more such surprises in our sphere; and, at this Plenum, we should be speaking of surprises. But nothing was said of them. You will see later where I am tending by stressing this particular aspect.

Although I have just expressed some doubts as to the wisdom of dividing verses into good and bad, the latter are nevertheless imaginable in another connection. Thus, comrades, I find myself in a somewhat similar period, and I am glad of it. For some time, I shall be writing badly from the point of view of my past until the moment when I can adapt myself to the novelty of the themes and the propositions which I wish to touch upon. My writing will be bad in many ways: from the artistic standpoint, because of this migration from position to position it will be necessary to achieve in a space charged with polemics and abstractions, a space of few images and inconcrete. It will be bad also from the point of view of the aims, for the sake of which this is being done, because I shall not speak in the common language of these themes which are common to us all. I shall not repeat what you have said, comrades, but shall dispute with you; and, since you are the majority, the dispute this time will be fatal, and its issue will be in your favor. And although I do not flatter myself here with any hopes, yet I have no choice: I am now living all this, and I cannot do otherwise. I printed two such poems in the January number of *Izvestia* January 1, 1936. They were written impulsively, the devil knows how, with a lightness permissible in the pure lyric, but impermissible on such themes which required artistic pondering. But that is the way it will be; I cannot overcome it; and, for some time to come, I shall write like a shoemaker, if you will forgive the expression.

Now another matter, comrades, which I have already touched upon slightly. The gigantomaniac upsets, in relation to which each one of us is but a gnat, have their consequences. But we ourselves, as members of a corporation, as atoms of the social fabric, are to blame as to some aspects of our literary stagnation. And we must not expect salvation by raising our efficiency, as has been said here. Art is unthinkable without risk and the self-sacrifice of soul. We must attain in practice to the freedom and daring of the imagination. Here, indeed, the surprises of which we spoke have their place. Do not expect directives in this matter. Only two of you, Becher and Svetlov, expressed themselves in this spirit.

Is the task of the administrators of the Writers' Union to instruct you to be daring? That is the task of each of us; it is our personal task. That is why each one of us has a mind and heart. I do not remember a decree among our laws which would forbid the exercise of genius; if there were such a decree, some of our leaders would have to forbid themselves. Thus, we have probably no less scope in the possibility of new ideas than in the remolding of old ideas.

And since I have already used the term "genius," I shall concentrate a while on this concept to avoid the onslaught of false arguments. In my opinion, genius is kin to the ordinary man. Moreover, a genius is the largest and rarest representative of that breed—its immortal expression. It represents the quantitative poles of the qualitatively homogeneous, exemplary mankind. The space between them is no void. The interval between them is filled with those "interesting people," those extraordinary persons, those third persons who, in my opinion, make up the crowd of the so-called average. This conviction I have already once expressed in connection with Mayakovsky in a book which I would now rewrite in a different way. But there I called him a large average man, comrades, an ordinary man such as this, who is not a genius in embryo, would make us all poorer. Upon this correct observation, religion has erected its false superstructure about the immortality of the soul; and only mediocrity, which has thought up long hair, violins and velvet jackets, separates the genius from the ordinary man.

Only in the understanding of this intermediate social environment, that is, in the distorting mirror of mediocrity, does it happen that if I write as best I can, then as a consequence I must do this or that. And, more specifically, let us say, that I must deny Demyan Biedny. I shall begin by stating that I prefer him to the majority of you. I shall say even more. You see, comrades, I am deeply indifferent to the component parts of the integral form, provided the latter is original and true, that is, I am not concerned whether it is artistic passion such as Balzac described it in "The Unknown Masterpiece" or some other passion that is the source of a large participation in life as long as there do not intrude between the author and his expression the intermediate links of imitation, false unusualness or bad taste—taste that is bad because it is mediocre taste. And

I will tell you, comrades, that Demyan Biedny is not only a historical figure of the Revolution in its decisive moments at the front and of militant communism, but he also remains for me to this day the Hans Sachs of our popular movement, whereas Mayakovsky, at whose genius I was amazed earlier than many of you and whom I loved to the point of adoration, bears no comparison in this sphere with the naturalness of Demyan Biedny's role. Where the one dissolves without sediment in the naturalness of a calling that is near to him, the other has found merely a point of application for only a portion of his measureless strength. I am looking at Mayakovsky from the historical perspective, comrades, and not from the point of view of poetic technique; and to avoid further distorted arguments, I shall end here.

[Stormy, prolonged applause]